WORSHIP'S JOURNEY

SIGNPOSTS TO THE PRESENCE OF GOD

KEVIN NORRIS

❀ Created with Vellum

DEDICATION

To David and Dale Garratt, pioneers in the Contemporary Worship Movement, who encouraged us to "lead the people to God" rather than just singing about him.

CONTENTS

INTRODUCTION

"I'd like to do that." The thought rushed through my mind as my eyes fixed on the young guitarist. It was the first time I had ever seen a group like this. In a basement filled with young people like myself, here was a guitar being used to accompany Christian songs. I had been brought up in the church in my homeland of New Zealand, and Sunday morning always meant organs and old hymns.

In high school, I was drawn to the whole rock music scene. I loved the Beatles, the Rolling Stones, they all used guitars. For me, at that time, guitars and Jesus did not go together. But here they were!

Something clicked inside of me. Was this God speaking to me?

I was captured by the enthusiasm and genuine faith of these new friends, and wanted to know what made the difference. It was not long before I bought my own guitar and learnt enough chords to begin playing along at our own newly fired-up church youth group.

That began a decades-long journey of leading others in praise and worship (as it was then called). When I started, I did not know much about what I was doing. But as I served, God taught me lessons that I have freely shared with others who love to worship. Eventually, I began leading Schools of Worship at Youth With A Mission's campus in Kona, Hawaii.

But what relevance do these lessons have today?

Looking at the past can give us perspective on where we are in God's story and even reveal our future. The Contemporary Worship Movement (CWM) emerged as a new era in music met the charismatic renewal amongst the post-war baby boomers. Some of this generation were newly converted, but others, like me, had grown up in traditional churches. Many of us were living a musical double life, loving rock music throughout the week, but singing old hymns with organ music in church on Sunday! But a new wave of spiritual life was using a wildly different, and often controversial, musical style in worship. From these beginnings the movement has matured, notably in the vast improvement in the quality of songwriting and music production. We're no longer forced to admit that the world's music is so much better.

So where are we at now?

As the 21st Century began, two movements emerged. One is a prayer movement combining with worship ministries sparking a new format of worship and prayer together. There has also been a movement toward reviving earlier Christian traditions and spiritual disciplines, such as liturgy, fasting, and *lectio divina* (meditative scripture reading). By both honoring the past and accepting recent moves of the Holy Spirit, this generation has the potential to take us even deeper in worship.

I see coming, a generation . . .

• whose motivation is towards pursuing the love of Jesus as their first priority, resting in his love, not concentrating on doing the right thing merely as an outward performance.

• who prioritize worship and prayer, practicing his presence, placing these as a priority and a foundation of their ministry activity.

• who are not afraid to incorporate spiritual disciplines in their pursuit of a deeper relationship with Jesus, things like fasting, Bible meditation, and memorization. They want more than a lone "quiet time."

• whose failures to live by Jesus' example are rare, and result in running towards God and not away from him.

• who are neither fearful of nor intoxicated with the supernatural. The miracle working power of God is becoming a normal part of life and ministry.

• who don't let denominational bias prevent them from learning from other streams in the Body of Christ.

• who are prepared and willing to follow God to the ends of the earth to share the love of Jesus' with the nations, no matter what the cost.

As this generation goes deeper in an authentic day-to-day friendship with Jesus, they will require worship experiences that reflect this greater depth. I have seen God pour out his Spirit in amazing ways in my lifetime, but there is more. In coming years, there will be new expressions that flow from burning hearts, but are not dependent on any particular music style. We'll see hearts, voices and actions making one sound of thanks, praise and worship. Fully authentic worship will rise up when loving hearts fully connect with the truths conveyed in the songs.

I see a people prepared to receive a new wave of God's Spirit, advancing the Kingdom of God through lives rooted in worship and prayer.

PREFACE

- WORSHIP AS A JOURNEY

Anyone called by God to lead worship in a church, youth group or ministry gathering will no doubt struggle at some point with these kinds of questions:

What are we trying to get these people to do?

Are we going anywhere?

If so, what is our goal and how do we get there?

Is there more to it than just setting a song list and practicing the music?

Are there some keys to seeing the response we hope for?

This book explores worship as a journey towards a distinctive encounter with God's presence, a journey of the heart that can affect every part of us.

But what do we mean by worship? Over many years, the way we have used the word *worship* has changed, and now it means different things in various contexts.

It entered the English language as a term for expressing honor and submission to someone higher, but as it began to be applied to Christian gatherings, it came to mean the worship service. Recently the word has come to represent the twenty or more minutes of singing, mostly at the beginning of a church service. But a further shift is taking place in which the word is being used to refer to an attitude of love and honor to God that can be applied to almost any activity we care to name. Hence the popular phrase "worship is a lifestyle."

This can get confusing so we need to be asking "what is worship?" This is an important question especially for worship leaders, but is helpful for every Christian. While scriptures such as 1Corinthians 10:31 and Colossians 3:17 confirm that whatever we do should be for God's glory, my study has led me to see worship as a special time set aside to meet with God and respond, either individually, or in a gathering. It is a time to come aside from the normal, everyday life with God, to a special sense of the Holy Spirit's presence as we focus on him alone.

I am also using worship to mean both a journey and its destination. This is not unfamiliar to us because we often refer to trips that way. "My Australia trip" usually means the whole journey, but it also tells us the destination.

For the average person air travel is still exciting. Even road trips. Whether we are on a vacation or visiting friends or family, the journey is something to look forward to with excitement. What is it about a journey that fascinates us?

I dare say it is the excitement of venturing beyond our comfort zones to discover new and special things. Worship can be seen as a special journey into the heart of God. On our journey, we need signposts that direct us towards our goal. We can be helped along the way by principles from the Bible. These biblical truths are applicable in every generation, in every nation or people group, and any type of church gathering. If we can sort out the important, unchanging truths about worship in the Bible, rather than clinging to cultural practices that are forever changing, we will provide a safer "ground zero" on which to build our worship culture in the future.

Our look at the journey follows three stages . . . . .

Our Heart – Fuel for the Journey

We begin by purifying the **motive** in our worship. We must ask ourselves what drives us? Why participate in worship? An ongoing, increasing love for Jesus is the fuel that keeps worship fresh and interesting. His life flows to us when we are connected in the Spirit through worship. Being genuine prevents lifeless, dry, and boring worship experiences. Boredom indicates a distancing from the heart of God.

Our Head – A Road Map to Guide Us

A worship leader must discover the **meaning** of worship. The Psalms, the Bible's songbook, provide a foundation for what we communicate to God. We also look specifically at the meaning of the words *thanksgiving, praise* and *worship*, as they are used throughout the Bible. We will see that speaking out meaningful truths about God, flowing from a genuine heart of love, moves us towards experiencing his presence.

Our Hands – Navigating our Worship

The worship leader must find a **method** of worship that works – So how do we do that? We tend to place far more importance on the worship style than God does. But when we discover and apply biblical principles, our worship teams are able to be more effective. Every nation, people, and generation has songs to sing, and God loves to hear them. The Bible places an emphasis on expressing a living relationship rather than conforming to outward, arbitrary, man-made rules. This section is directed more towards worship leaders, but remains helpful for all those wanting to experience the presence of God in worship.

PART I

FUEL FOR THE JOURNEY

1

SHIFTING SANDS OR SOLID ROCK

"Why have you brought the devil's music into the church?" one of the more conservative members of our church protested. Our youth group had been given free rein in taking an evening service in our church. Our worship band had included a drum set along with our usual guitars to add a little more punch to the songs.

The horrified elder challenged us, "Don't you know that rock music is the devil's music?"

"How come?" we replied.

I needed some answers, but the elder's lectures on the evils of rock music were unconvincing. We were told on more than one occasion that "scientific" research proved that playing rock music to plants caused them to wilt, while classical music made the plants thrive. We heard how the drum beats of rock music were the same ones used in Africa by witchdoctors to call up demons. Finally, we were alerted to the danger of imitating "worldly music and the notorious lifestyles of ungodly rock musicians."

Their arguments appeared to make sense, and we certainly

did not want to emulate the lifestyle of rock musicians, but something inside of me could not quite accept that a whole music style could be branded as evil. We began to experience something similar to what many indigenous peoples had suffered through years of missionary misunderstandings. We were being told we could not use our own instruments or music styles for worship.

I remember going to my first contemporary Christian music concert. I was so excited. It was truly Christian – pointing our hearts to God -- and yet the music sounded like my generation. It did not sound like the devil's music at all. But eventually those words began haunting me again. Mature Christian teachers I respected kept saying, "Rock music is from the devil." What was the answer?

Could I like rock music and still be a good Christian? Could we sing these new upbeat songs in worship? Could electric guitars and drums be used to honor God?

I found the answer in a book by Steve Miller called *The Contemporary Christian Music Debate*. Steve outlined the history of church music, explaining that debates over music were not new, they had happened before. Over the centuries, church music had often found itself alienated from the outside world, forming a "stained glass barrier" between the church and those outside its walls.

Bold innovators, like Isaac Watts in England, introduced new forms of music, challenging the established styles. His new hymns were vehemently opposed by the guardians of the status quo. They protested that we should never sing the words of a mere mortal man to such a holy God. Singing metrical Psalms (Psalms set to music) was the accepted form of church music at that time.

William Booth, founder of the Salvation Army, went even further by using tunes from the bars while changing the lyrics. He wanted to reach people in London who would never enter a church, so he used music they recognized. Opponents criticized his use of "worldly" music but General Booth decided to plunder the devil's music and use it for the Kingdom of God. History would say he succeeded.

As I read these fascinating stories, the revelation sank in. "That's what is happening now." Steve's book encouraged me to read more about the history of church music. New music always seemed to accompany spiritual renewals, but any innovation would face strong opposition before becoming accepted. I realized that I was in the midst of one of these so-called "worship wars."

"What is wrong with the old hymns?" the elders would ask. "They are more theologically correct and full of meaning. These new choruses are shallow and trite." I didn't even know what trite meant then, but I got the idea when others added, "Choruses are musically inferior and not worthy of singing in church."

I am sad to say, such disagreements continue to this day. Biblical truths about worship seemed clouded behind the smoke screen of personal preference in musical styles. Despite the conflict, huge changes in church worship services have taken place over the past decades. In thousands of churches, 200-year-old hymns have been replaced by contemporary music; the once-formal dress of suits and ties (and hats for women) have given way to a more casual approach. Many welcomed this change; others still warn of the dangers.

~

THE SHIFT in church culture was never more apparent to me than on a Sunday, many years later, when I stood next to my parents in their small Methodist church in New Zealand. I thought, *These church services haven't changed in 35 years.* Being there took me back to my days as a child standing with my family, holding the Methodist hymn book, attempting to sing the words with the accompanying pipe organ. Then we would sit down on hard wooden pews and listen to the sermon.

I could see the enormous contrast between the services I experienced as a child and the worship I was now involved with. Church culture was moving fast, yet many churches like my parents' clung to centuries-old music traditions. Could we both be right in the way we worshipped? Jesus, whom we both worshipped was still the same, and the Bible, which we both revered still said the same things. So what is the difference?

My experiences in world missions had taught me that Christian worship often reflects aspects of the surrounding culture. Cultures change, and rapid change such as we have had in the last century breeds uncertainty and insecurity.

Fortunately, in God's family, we have an anchor in the storm of constant change. The Word of God keeps us grounded by providing unchanging principles for all of life, and it has plenty to say about worship and song.

When lovers of the "old time religion" clashed with contemporary innovators in the 1970s, there was never a better time to reconsider our worship culture in the light of biblical principles. But rather than looking to the Bible for guidance, most arguments were fueled by fiery protestations of personal preference. In other words, it amounted to "what I like is the way it should be!"

One of the most important questions in the shifting sands of church culture is: What aspects of church life (such as worship style) are OK to safely change, and what must remain the same? Sadly, this question hasn't always been answered satisfactorily. As the church, we have spent so much time arguing about the format of worship, while God seems more interested in principles than methods. The Bible gives no indication that any style of music is preferred, but it does say that whatever we sing or speak in worship must come from the heart.

When I first began playing guitar in my youth group, sometimes we would bring our music style into the main church service. "It is too loud" was often the protest. Then I discovered verses in the Bible that encouraged us to sing with a loud voice, or even shout to the Lord! Should I follow people's preferences or did the Bible give me guidelines?

So I began a quest, a search for meaning and truth concerning principles of worship. If God was more interested in principle than methods, what are those biblical signposts that should guide our worship practices?

Let's see what the Bible can show us.

2

THE JOURNEY - WHERE TO?

After a number of years leading worship, a thought kept popping into my mind, "Worship is a journey, a journey of the heart." Could this be a helpful way of looking at worship? Could the concept of a journey be a framework on which we construct our worship services? I began to see language of movement in the Bible, along with a set of conditions, protocols, signposts for the journey. There seemed to be a reason why our praise and worship times had a sense of flow, of direction. I began to see wording in scripture that indicated movement towards God. For example:

> *Therefore, brothers, since we have confidence to* ***enter*** *the holy places by the blood of Jesus, by the new and* ***living way*** *that he opened for us* ***through*** *the curtain, that is, through his flesh, and since we have a great priest over the house of God, let us* ***draw near*** *with a true heart – Hebrews 10:19-22*

> *And without faith it is impossible to please him, for whoever would* ***draw***

__near__ to God must believe that he exists and that he rewards those who seek him. – Hebrews 11:6

Let us then with confidence __draw near__ to the throne of grace, that we may receive mercy and find grace to help in time of need. – Hebrews 4:16

Let us __come into__ his presence with thanksgiving; – Psalm 95:2

__Enter__ his gates with thanksgiving – Psalm 100:4

Who shall __ascend__ the hill of the Lord? – Psalm 24:3

The phrase "draw near" implies there are times we can be closer to God than we normally experience. Other words like *enter, through,* and *way* also speak of a direction.

A Journey into a Special Place with God

Where is the journey of worship taking us?

Whether it is using an ancient path of a liturgical communion service, or lifting hands in praise to the sound of contemporary worship music, the goal is the same – a special meeting with God.

In the Old Testament, God's presence was clearly recognized in the Holy of Holies, the inner sanctuary of the tabernacle. God's glory radiated there, there was no natural lighting, it must have been impressive.

For the Hebrew people, the Holy of Holies was *the* special place of God's presence. The word *holy* means set apart, distinct, different from the ordinary. This was a unique place above all other special places. The biblical Hebrew way of indicating a superlative can be seen in phrases like King of kings, Song of songs, Lord of lords etc., Jesus is the King above all other kings. Solomon's song is the Song above all other songs, Jesus is the Lord above all other lords etc. The Holy of Holies was like no other location, it was the most holy, the holiest of all.

Although God is everywhere, he often chooses to demonstrate his presence in particular ways that are unmistakable.

Our lives are spent mostly in the ordinary, common activities of life, but then we have special times, birthdays, celebrations, and special events. Married couples have special places, special times together.

Our group worship times can be like that – some of the most powerful or tender encounters with God happen during worship. We may all have individual touches from God as we meet together, but something amazing happens when there is an overall sense of the powerful presence of God. Some might say that feelings are not necessary, but what kind of relationship exists if you don't feel anything. I have no doubt that the priests who entered the Holy of Holies felt his presence. It had to stir within them feelings of awe, conviction, joy, love, and holy fear.

So How Do We Approach God?

Moses' tabernacle was a picture of a journey into the unusual presence of God. As priests approached, there were clear conditions that had to be met. There were severe consequences for disobeying God's protocols for entry into his presence.

The tabernacle set up by Moses still has something to teach us today about how to draw near to God. Some may argue that Old Testament practices have no relevance today. But we must remember that Moses' tabernacle was a copy of heaven's tabernacle which has eternal meaning.

In describing the tabernacle worship, the writer of Hebrews says, *"This is an illustration pointing to the present time" (Hebrews 9:9a NLT)*. Because it is an Old Testament picture of entering God's presence, we need to see what might be applicable today, what changed in the New Testament, and what has remained the same.

The book of Hebrews teaches that we no longer have to regularly sacrifice animals to cover our sin because Jesus was a "once and for all" sacrifice that allows us to be completely forgiven and cleansed. That is the part that has changed. The way is now open to all who love Jesus.

What remains the same? In the Old Testament we are taught that we must be clean to enter his presence.

> *Who shall ascend the hill of the Lord?*
> *And who shall stand in his holy place?*
> *He who has* ***clean hands and a pure heart,***
> *who does not lift up his soul to what is false*
> *and does not swear deceitfully. – Psalms 24:3-4*

This qualification hasn't changed. It is repeated in the New Testament. God still looks at our heart.

> *"let us draw near with a* ***true heart*** *in full assurance of faith, with our* ***hearts sprinkled clean*** *from an evil conscience and our bodies washed with pure water." – Hebrews 10:22*

The requirements for blood sacrifices are now no longer necessary, and thankfully, we have a way to be cleansed by receiving the forgiveness that Jesus offers because of his death and resurrection. God's requirements for approaching him are not outward conforming to rules, but inward qualities of the heart. The way into his presence is now a **journey of the heart**. We interact with God in the spiritual realm, even though we may sing, dance or clap as an outward demonstration.

When we are getting to know someone, we follow cultural protocols. When we'd like to go deeper in a relationship, especially a romantic one, there are accepted procedures that obviously vary with cultures. The most significant step to take a romantic relationship deeper is a marriage proposal. That simple question and answer moved my relationship with Liz to a whole new level. It shifted our hearts closer in a way that's difficult to explain. I loved her before, but after that pledge, we entered into a deeper trust and intimacy. Today, even small acts of love continue to draw us closer.

It is true that God is with us every moment of the day, but there are also times when we might feel particularly close to him, often it is during worship. Have you experienced times like that? Do these situations occur in a random fashion, or are there things we can do to welcome the presence of the Holy Spirit in such a way that our experience is unmistakably different from normal? The Bible tells us there are things we should do. These Old Testament verses still apply today because they involve our hearts . . .

Let us ***come into his presence*** *with thanksgiving; let us make a joyful noise to him with songs of praise! – Psalm 95:2*

> ***Enter his gates*** *with thanksgiving, and his courts with praise! Give thanks to him; bless his name! – Psalm 110:4*

Other Old Testament worship practices have changed because of Jesus's sacrificial death. We don't need the blood sacrifices of animals to enter God's special presence anymore . . .

> *. . . let us draw near with a* ***true heart*** *in full assurance of* ***faith****, with our* ***hearts sprinkled clean*** *from an evil conscience and our bodies* ***washed with pure water****. – Hebrews 10:19-22*

> *And without* ***faith*** *it is impossible to please him, for whoever would draw near to God must* ***believe*** *that he exists and that he rewards those who seek him. – Hebrews 11:6*

Hebrews 10:19-22 shows us that now the requirements to enter his presence are a clean conscience, honesty, and hearts of faith. Peter's first epistle adds spiritual sacrifices which might include thanks and praise . . .

> *As you* ***come to him****, a living stone rejected by men but in the sight of God chosen and precious, you yourselves like living stones are being built up as a spiritual house, to be a holy priesthood, to offer* ***spiritual sacrifices*** *acceptable to God through Jesus Christ. – 1 Peter 2:4-5*

> *Through him then let us continually offer up a* ***sacrifice of praise*** *to God, that is, the fruit of* ***lips that acknowledge his name.*** *– Hebrews 13:15*

Drawing near to God in the New Testament involves a journey of the heart. We do what is necessary to prepare our hearts to experience God's presence. As we approach him, his love reaches out to us. Movie directors know how to move our hearts. Have you ever walked out of a movie with your heart stirred in some way? In worship we can see our heart tenderized and warmed by God's presence, receiving new hope, new vision, healing or by letting his truth touch whatever our situation requires.

New Testament Requirements to Enter God's Presence

We can see from the above verses that there are new qualifications to enter the spiritual "holy of holies" that are different from the Old Testament requirements of animal sacrifices.

1. An honest, genuine heart

Our worship is only acceptable to God if we mean what we say, a "true heart." We may also need to deal with whatever is troubling our heart, by pouring out to God and receiving his comfort.

2. Confidence that God will welcome us – that is, faith.

Our hearts can be moved by thinking about and professing **thanks** for what Jesus has done on the cross to make it possible to experience his presence. Thanks builds faith as we gain confidence that God receives our worship.

3. A Clean Conscience

Unconfessed sin in our lives becomes a barrier for us to be wholehearted in our love. This is true in our earthly relationships - it is difficult to be intimate or deeply connected with a friend when there are lingering tensions caused by small irritations or more serious wounding.

4. Offerings of Praise

No longer animal sacrifices, but offerings of praise, proclaiming the goodness of God!

These are not merely outward performances, they are expressions from the deepest part of our being, which is why worship is not only a journey of the mind. We reveal our hearts and we listen to hear God's. So where does the journey begin? The Bible points us inward.

3

WHEN THE FIRE DIES DOWN

KEEPING WORSHIP FRESH

What makes worship inspiring and meaningful for you? When the music is upbeat and the people are enthusiastic, it feels good to be a part of it. But if we are really honest with ourselves, there are times when we are more excited about going to the latest movie or watching the big game.

What is it that keeps worship fresh week after week, year after year? Is it new songs, better arrangements, more skilled musicians, louder sound systems? Or is it new worship styles which include all the senses, sights, sounds and smells, maybe recapturing some of the historical practices like incense or ancient music?

We are often told that worship is a choice. This often works, but what happens when even choosing does not do it for us?

I have discovered that working on the outward forms of worship, although helpful, can never take the place of making sure our hearts are continually rekindled with a fresh, flourishing love for God. If we want to keep our worship invigorating, then our hearts must be kept alive with vibrant love. Our love for God is like a fire:

> *"love is strong as death , jealousy is fierce as the grave. Its flashes are flashes of fire, the very flame of the LORD."* — Song of Songs 8:6

When the heart has grown colder, no amount of choosing to get into the worship will light the flame. Our worship becomes more fake as time goes on and nothing changes.

One of the highlights of camping with my family was building a campfire. Our hearts are like that campfire. If we don't throw on logs occasionally, the fire slowly dies down. When it settles, we put on a couple of logs, but nothing much happens for a little while. If we blow on the embers under the logs, suddenly it bursts into flame and burns brightly for a time. If we leave a fire by itself, it burns, then glows, then fades and eventually dies out. We are left with black ashes, and sometimes a little unburned wood that escaped the heat. No more flames, just the memory of what it used to be like, the warmth long gone.

We may be serving God and persevering through all kinds of hardships, but if we fail to stoke the fire of our love, it fades. As committed followers of Jesus, our greatest temptation may not be falling back into a sinful lifestyle, but like the Pharisees in Jesus' time, the danger comes when we appear religious while our love for God fades.

Like a dying campfire, we grow cold slowly. If it happened quickly we would notice it, but because it dims so slowly, it is almost unnoticeable. That's why it is so dangerous. It is the enemy's ploy to draw us away from God. He knows he can not tempt us away quickly with things of the world. We have learned how those things don't satisfy. We are tempted to believe the lie that staying loyal in a church body, means we will be OK.

But faithfulness is not enough! When we face the Lord at judgment day, I don't think he will ask us whether we have been loyal to a church or home group. He will ask us, "Do you love me?"

If our love for God begins to fade, we begin to look for some other kind of love apart from God. The enemy can sense our lack of love and he puts temptations in front of us that often cause us to fall into sin. But because we are in the church we tend to keep these things secret. Unconfessed sin will continue to deaden our connection with God. Worship becomes just an outward performance as we play the church game of convincing our Christian friends that we are doing fine while guilt tears us up inside.

A while back during a season when busyness had cooled my spiritual passion, I was reading in the book of Revelation where the angel speaks to the seven churches. I got to the second chapter, to the church at Ephesus. Even though it was spoken to a church a long time ago, I felt the words were speaking directly to me. I read "I know your works." I thought, cool, God sees my hard work for him. I continued to read. God sees my patience, my perseverance – it felt good to know that God sees that I have served him faithfully. But then I read "You have left your first love."

Surely not me, Lord, I thought. "Is that really you saying that." God did not argue with me, he simply challenged me with a thought flashing into my mind, "Kevin, what are you doing to get to know me better?" I was rocked! So I stumbled over my thoughts looking for an answer. "Well, I read and study the

Bible," but then I realized that I was spending almost all my Bible time studying to teach others. Well then, I pray, sometimes. "Oh dear, I guess I just pray for things I need, for success in ministry and for others. It looks like, Lord, that I'm not actually doing anything right now to get to know you better." I had trouble believing it was true, but it was. Then I felt the heart of God reply, "Won't you just spend some time with me, without thinking about ministry to others?"

It hit me that my love for God had dimmed. Sure I had been faithful, but I had to conclude that if I was not doing anything to get to know him better, then my love was indeed growing cold.

Around that time, I met some people who radiated passion for Jesus. It was so convicting. I felt like a bad Christian, but then it also gave me hope. I realized there is more I can learn, a deeper relationship is really possible. If they have found it, so can I.

What would we think if we were married, and all the other marrieds were stuck in the same level of love for one another, or worse, they were growing tired and bored with one another? Seeing older couples who are still growing in their love is a great encouragement for younger ones.

If you are married or hope to be in the future, then you'll no doubt want to grow in love for your partner. Most married couples will tell you that it does not just happen, it takes work to keep that love firing. If we avoid effort in getting closer, then we will begin to slowly drift apart, there is no middle ground. I heard of couples married for over 25 years, then getting divorced. "How could this happen?" I thought. Didn't they love one another more as time went on? Unfortunately not! If we don't stoke the fire, it will cool down gradually, sometimes without us noticing. This fade-out that happens with couples can also happen to our relationship with God.

We either push further in our relationship with God, or we end up trying to live on the past memories of his love. We can easily fall into dry religious patterns of worship that fail to satisfy the deep longings of the heart. We sing the songs, but the fun has gone out of it. We keep it up because deep down we know it is the right thing to do. We occasionally get pumped by cool worship music and a hyped-up crowd, but when we lie down to sleep at night, we find we are still empty. It is a sure sign we are getting religious! Our hearts are growing cold.

Any person or group that puts real effort into getting to know Jesus and his love will begin to discover life, creativity and joy in their expressions of praise and worship. More skilled musicians will give you better music, which is pleasing, but even that can grow stale. But when a group of people stoke the fire of love for Jesus, then their worship takes on new life, greater passion, and there is no place for boredom in that kind of atmosphere.

So what are these logs that we throw on the fire of our love for God? What makes them burst into flame?

4

LOGS THAT KEEP THE FIRE F

Intimacy with God in worship can be cultivated as we seek a deeper relationship with him. There are practical steps we can take on this journey, steps that take us into the throne room of God. The Bible encourages us to "seek God," which requires action on our part. Growth in God does not just happen.

Genuine experiences with God

Think of a good friend of yours. What made them a friend? Probably spending time with them, supporting them in times of need, and having fun times together. In the same way, we need experiences with God. He is more than just an idea, he is a person we can get to know and enjoy. The Bible is full of stories of men and women who had close experiences with God. Sure, there are times when we don't feel close to God, but unless we have had some deep connecting points with the Lord, I doubt whether we have really got to know him.

As a child I was taught about God and never really doubted he existed, but I did not "meet" him in a real way until I made a n to follow Jesus as a 13-year-old. But as a high schooler, a widening gap between my church culture and the social e to which I was being drawn.

By this time I was part of a youth group that loved hanging out together, but on Sunday morning we could not wait for the service to be over so we could plan the rest of the day's fun. On one of our organized fun trips to a beach, a couple of girls asked me if I wanted to go to a prayer meeting the following Saturday night. What? A prayer meeting! Saturday night was for fun, and prayer meetings in my experience were just the opposite. But they were really pretty girls, so I said yes, I'd join them.

I descended the stairs to a basement room filled with other teenagers. I thought "Wow, this is different!" They sang with infectious enthusiasm, clapped along to the music, and spoke of answered prayer. They actually looked like they were enjoying themselves, and it all fascinated me.

As I hung out with these new friends, I found out what made them so happy and bouncy. They had asked Jesus to fill them with the Holy Spirit, just like in the Book of Acts. I had been warned about people who were getting excited about God. But that's just what I needed. I was captured by Paul's encouragement to the Corinthian church to go after all the gifts that the Holy Spirit was giving. I wanted what these others had. They talked about God as though he was a real person; they prayed like they believed God heard them. It was probably the first time I heard people say that God answered their specific prayers. They had a contagious joy that I hadn't seen in the church where I had grown up. I longed for an experience of God like they had, and God answered my prayer.

One night at one of these gatherings, I asked for prayer that I would experience the fire of the Holy Spirit. I was changed. I met the reality of the presence and power of God; it was no longer just an idea in my head. It was real. I had experienced a touch from God that was more than just a warm feeling or peace of mind. It was powerful, and why not; if God is powerful, why couldn't we experience some of it? I certainly did. I started to enjoy the songs they were singing, the words now meant a lot more. When I sang "I love You Lord" the words matched my heart.

Friends who stoke the fire

It was not just me that was changed. Gradually, most of our youth group had experienced God in some way or another, and we loved getting together to sing and pray. We'd come a long way from that group of teenagers that only wanted to go on outings. We encouraged one another, and grew spiritually as a group. That's what God wants. He wants us to keep being fired up by stoking each other's fire. When you take a burning log out of the fire, it cools down quickly, it needs the heat of the fire to keep it burning well. We need each other. We need to be part of a group that wants to grow in God, a group who actively looks for ways to go deeper in his love. If we are in a place where people avoid making an effort to know God, then we will most likely cool off.

Before Liz and I were married, my friend Steve and I spent a lot of time together. He would challenge me, get me thinking and make me laugh. He enriched my life and we both grew in our relationship with God because we provoked each other to go deeper. When we find friends who love God, we'll help keep each other's fire burning.

Loving to read the Bible

Relationships grow as we spend time communicating on a heart-to-heart basis. It is like that with God. He can speak to us in a number of ways, but one sure way is through his Word, the Bible. As we find how much God loves us by reading the Bible, we can't help but love him more.

Discovering the depths of his love fuels the fire of our love. I have often thought about what it is about my wife that I love the most. Is it how she looks or her kindness? Is it her faithfulness and dependability? Is it her abilities at work around the house? I appreciate all those things. But the thing that I like most, the thing that touches me more than anything else, is that she loves and respects me. That really gets me deep down! When we read the Bible and keep seeing more of God's incredible, persistent, forgiving love for us personally, we find ourselves loving him more.

I am beginning to learn to read the Bible as a love letter from God. I remember when Liz and I were engaged, our roles in YWAM meant we spent most of the time apart. During that time we would write letters to each other; this was before emails and social networking! When a letter arrived amongst a bundle of other mail, I would recognize her writing and grab it from the pile. I could not get to read it quickly enough. I loved seeing those words, "Dear Kevin!" I would read about what she'd been doing, but what I most loved to read was how she missed me, how much she loved me and how she was looking forward to the next time we would be together. I would read the lines over and over. I would put the letter in my pocket and bring it out later. No one had to tell me I should make time to read the letters! I wondered why reading the Bible was not like this. Could it be my love for God was not as exciting? Possibly. Could God's love be exciting? It must be. Maybe I could find more of his thoughts towards me in the pages. So I began to look, and a life of discovery continues. Probably the most important message to us in the Bible is that God loves us and the depth and reality of this love is there for us to uncover by reading and study.

Enjoying time alone with God

To build a friendship, we must spend time talking and doing things together. As we get to know each other better, we begin to share joys, hopes and dreams as well as the hard times. It is like that with God. We get to know him by talking to him and hearing from him. He is a God who speaks and wants us to speak with him.

For a long time I wondered why I struggled with disciplining my life to make sure I had daily "quiet time" with God. The time-honored method is to get up early in the morning, read three chapters of the Bible a day, pray, worship, etc. Why did I find this so difficult? Then I found out discipline is not enough. When your heart is burning with the love of God, it becomes something that you just want to do! We still need discipline, but it is a lot easier when the logs are burning!

When a guy sees a girl who's worth getting to know better, what should he do? He could hang out in a group, but he will never really know if she is "the one" until he spends some time alone with her. Does he have to discipline himself to spend time with her? Not if a flame of love has been kindled. A few years after marriage, this couple might find they're not spending as much quality time together. Then they need discipline to throw logs on the fire of their love. But it is not a difficult thing.

When our fire is burning, it is not a chore to find time to be alone with God. We remember that we actually enjoy hearing from God, sensing his love, and sharing our burdens. Time alone with one another, in a marriage or in our relationship with God, keeps the fire burning. Throw another log on the fire of your love; spend some quality time together!

But how? What will bring you closer together? First of all, just show up. Be proactive. You might want to go for a walk, sit on a chair, kneel or lay on your face or listen to worship music. Some like to meditate on Scripture, sing, pray, recount blessings, express thanks, always listening for the voice of the Holy Spirit. Do whatever you find brings you closer to God. We may have heard of many "quiet time" schemes, but following someone else's method may work for a time, but eventually we find ourselves looking for something more rewarding. If we truly want to enjoy our time with God, we have to find the most fruitful way for us by trying different approaches.

But There's a War Going On . . .

The flesh is at war with the Spirit. Our fleshly desires show up when we know what we should be doing but we just haven't got the energy. Whatever we feed will grow. We have to feed our spirit while denying these natural impulses. What would you rather miss, a meal or a prayer meeting?

The way to get free from sins of the flesh is not to put all our efforts into fighting the temptation. The more we concentrate on resisting, the more we fall. The way to freedom is to make choices to pursue God rather than our own desires for food, entertainment or pleasure. When loving God captures our heart more than the sin, the temptation falls away.

To feed our spirits we must voluntarily add activities that help us grow. It also helps to restrict things that compete for attention. For example, fasting is a denial of something that has a strong pull on our lives. It also could be fasting time on our phone, whatever is a strong desire. These desires don't need any encouraging, they come at us naturally. Anything that has a place of power in our hearts is called an idol. What part of your flesh do you struggle with? Give him the opportunity to truly satisfy that need by giving it up.

Growing in love for God . . .

I once heard a teacher say that we can't make loving Jesus the number one goal of our lives without a lifestyle of fasting. That thought challenged me, so I set a fasting goal that I thought might work. Fasting food is not fun, you get hungry! But I really wanted to kill the flesh to increase my desire for God. A few weeks later I suddenly noticed an area of failure had completely disappeared. I was a bit confused because I believed that to get rid of sin I had to repent and fight hard to resist temptation. Repenting is right, but this time God wanted to show me the weakness of my will power. Fasting increased his power in my life and unlocked his gift of grace and freedom. I was therefore convinced about the value of fasting, and have continued.

Then after a few years, I was reading my Bible one morning and suddenly realized something was different. I had changed. No longer was reading the Bible a chore. It was a delight. The words came alive to me so much more than before. I learned that I could not make myself enjoy God's Word, I could not work up hunger and thirst for God. I just had to put myself in the position to receive his gift of a changed heart by feeding my spirit and not my flesh.

Once a young man came to me for relationship advice. He lamented that he was in love with a particular girl but was getting nowhere. I asked him if he had talked to her, but he hadn't. I am not sure you can even say you are in love if you have never talked together. My advice was that he would have to actually DO something if he wanted to get to know her. There may have been a number of different courses of action I could have advised, but one thing was sure, it was unlikely that anything would happen if he remained inactive. I believe this principle also works in our relationship with God; if you want to grow closer to God, you have to DO something.

It is not that we can earn our way into loving or being loved by God more, but he does ask us to seek him with all our hearts. I am persuaded that even though we do something, it is really God that causes the shift in our hearts. Even hunger for God is a gift of God.

When someone shares with us how they love God passionately, we are either thinking that it is good news or we fall into "I tried that before, and it didn't work" or " that's nice for them, but I don't think I am good enough."

Something lit up inside of me when I heard that there could be more, I might really be able to love God more than I do now.

I am convinced we need both desire and discipline to go deeper in God. Other words for desire are hunger, passion or motivation. Discipline means structure, schedule, plan, determination, will or choice. For some, it may be that discipline sparks desire, but for others desire is needed to get us started. We need both. Without a plan, we wander about casually, and desire quickly fades. Without desire, our plan or schedule can become dry and boring, or we may not even get started, we are just not motivated.

If you feel something stirring in your heart, a holy dissatisfaction with your relationship with Jesus, you know in your heart there is more, then make a choice now to DO something.

I want to invite you right now to tell God that you want more and you'd like to know him on a deeper level. Pray a prayer or write down your thoughts with words something like this . . .

"God, I am not satisfied with where I am at in my relationship with you. I know there is more but I am just not very hungry. Please help me, give me a hunger and thirst for more of you. I know I struggle to spend time with you, even though I want to. My heart is willing, but my flesh is weak, please help me."

Jesus saw spiritual thirst in a woman who spoke with him in a conversation recorded in the gospel of John. As the woman spoke about worship, Jesus began teaching her one of the most important lessons, it is not our method of worship that God is looking at. It is whether we are genuine in our declarations of love and loyalty to him. Let's join the story.

5

JESUS TEACHES ON WORSHIP

There is very little record of Jesus teaching about worship, so what is written in John 4 is particularly significant. Jesus talked to a Samaritan woman at Jacob's Well about living water. He revealed things about her past that shocked her. After calling Jesus a prophet, she launched into a discussion on worship.

Believing Jesus to be some sort of prophet, she brought up a controversy that separated Jews and Samaritans. Where was the "right" place to worship, in Jerusalem or nearby at Mount Gerizim? Why did she mention this? What was she really saying?

I have heard teachers say that she changed the subject because the conversation was getting too personal! The gospel text does not say why she changed the subject. We can make educated guesses, but these are usually influenced by our own culture and way of thinking. I am not convinced that she was trying to divert attention away from her sin by changing the subject.

I want to suggest another possible explanation of why she

asked this question, based on historical considerations. Our interpretation of her motive will affect the way we understand what Jesus said about worship. How was Jesus' explanation an answer to her problem of where to worship?

Many commentators emphasize the sinfulness of this woman and are fairly negative in their assessment of her words and actions. But consider the culture of the time. Almost all the power in deciding a Jewish or Samaritan divorce was with the man. It is likely she was "put away," or dumped, by five men previously. We don't know why, but it might change the way we think of this woman. It is possible that Jesus began the conversation about living water because he sensed she was wounded by abuse and multiple rejections from men. Maybe it was her fault, maybe not. She appeared thirsty for love, and Jesus knew how to connect her with the kind of love that would never disappoint or reject her. Jesus was compassionate to sinners, especially ones who had suffered injustice, and my feeling is this was such a woman.

She had probably been taught that to connect with God, she must worship, and as a Samaritan, Mount Gerizim was the place to do it. Now, while conversing with a Jew who had just revealed deep, dark secrets about her life, she probably realized this man could help her connect with God. So she asked which mountain was the "right" place to worship. In other words, what kind of worship was acceptable to God? Her statement about worship looks to me like an honest request for Jesus' input, since she recognized him as a Jewish prophet.

From the time she was a little girl, it is likely she would have heard reasons why the Samaritans were right and the Jews were wrong. Does this sound familiar? So maybe now she was not so sure that her Samaritan way was right. She was asking how someone like this could tell her things about her life unless he truly could hear from God? Who's right? Where is the right place to worship?

Today we would ask, what is the "right" way to worship? Is it liturgical, following a prayer book, is it spontaneous and free-flowing, is it contemporary songs, is it older hymns? These questions have been debated for centuries. It might help to have an answer from God! The Samaritan woman recognized a prophet in front of her, so she asked.

Jesus' answer was profound and equally meaningful for us today. Jesus led her away from the outward forms of worship as the measure of God's acceptance. Some say that Jesus was redefining worship here by saying worship is only an inward attitude. I feel that he was simply showing what is important to God about the *way* we worship. He is looking for the "true" worshipers. The word "true" in Greek, *alethinos,* means genuine, authentic, real, "what you see is what you get." It is the inward heart that God looks at to test the genuineness of our worship. The outward forms we demonstrate may or may not reflect our heart. If they don't, God calls it false worship. It is still worship, but he does not want to hear it!

It was not new teaching though; God had spoken in the Old Testament that he looks on the heart, not on the outward.

> *I hate, I despise your feasts, and I take no delight in your solemn assemblies.*
>
> *Even though you offer me your burnt offerings and grain offerings, I will not accept them; and the peace offerings of your fattened animals, I will not look upon them.*
>
> *Take away from me the noise of your songs; to the melody of your harps I will not listen. - Amos 5:21-23*

> *The Lord says: "These people come near to me with their mouth and honor me with their lips, but their hearts are far from me. Their worship of me is based on merely human rules they have been taught - Isaiah 29:13 (NIV)*

The woman's question was not "what is worship?" It was "what method of worship is acceptable?" Jesus' answer, therefore, was not to redefine worship, as it was already understood, but rather to explain the kind of worship he accepts. He is looking for worship that truly reflects the inward heart attitude of the worshiper. In other words, if we sing "I love you, Lord," God looks at our heart to see whether we really mean that. Ladies, if a guy says to you, "I love you," you are probably going to check out whether he really means that. God is doing exactly the same thing when he listens to us singing his praises or proclaiming our love or commitment.

God is not so much interested in how well we sing, whether we are following modern or ancient traditions, whether we are dancing and clapping or being quiet. These things are not as important to God as being genuine. Are we really meaning what we are saying or singing?

Let's consider the words of our songs before we open our mouths, and ask ourselves whether we mean them. Let's be "true" worshipers who mean what we say and do.

6

GETTING REAL

The opposite of genuine worship is fake or hypocritical worship, saying one thing, but not really meaning it. Jesus called the Pharisees hypocrites because they loved praise from men more than pleasing God. They tried to impress people with their public displays of devotion that did not at all reflect the true nature of their hearts.

Jesus likened them to whitewashed tombs, nice on the outside, but dead on the inside, a damning analysis of their true motivation. In Matthew 23, Jesus rebukes them with possibly the strongest language recorded in the New Testament. He calls the Pharisees "a brood of vipers!" I think today's movie censors might give that scene a PG or PG13 rating. In any case, we can be sure that God is not pleased when we sing one thing and mean another. Honesty and genuineness are what he is looking for.

It is really easy for us to join in the words of a song without even thinking what we are communicating or whether we actually mean it.

It is easy for us to criticize the Pharisees for their hypocrisy, but I am sure there is a little Pharisee in all of us. Most of us like to look good and we like to sound good too! It is tempting for church musicians, in their pride, to spend more time working on sounding good musically, rather than considering whether the lyrics will truly reflect their hearts or those they are leading.

If you are like me, you have occasionally felt uncomfortable as you watched worship leaders and sensed they were a bit fake. It is so tempting for us as worship leaders to learn tricks from rock stars for pumping up a crowd. True worshipers quickly see through the showbiz antics. We get turned off and long for simple honesty.

I once was asked to teach on worship at a church and, as part of the training, I was asked to lead their worship team for an evening service. I gathered the worship team for preparation and surprised many of them by sitting down to pray about what we should do. They were not used to that, but they joined me in asking God for guidance in the service. One of the singers thought we should sing the old song "Jesus loves me, this I know, for the Bible tells me so." Now that's not the trendiest of songs to sing with young people, and we expected a mostly younger gathering that evening. But seeing it was a training time, I thought it was best to go with what they felt God was saying. It did not take much to practice the music, as it is a fairly simple song, and everyone seemed to know it. So we practiced it along with a few other songs.

We began the evening by singing a few songs on our list, then I thought we better sing "Jesus loves me." Until that time there was not much response from the people, but as we began to sing that simple song, it seemed like God began touching people's hearts in a noticeable way. I invited those present to begin praying for one another, and there was a sweet presence of the Lord in the room. It was a lesson to me and to the worship team, that obeying God and being real was far more important than trying to look and sound trendy or cool.

In these times image is important to many of us. We have to remember that God is looking right past these outward considerations, right into our hearts. It is a challenge to give more consideration to our heart condition than to how we appear when our society is yelling at us "image is everything!"

That little bit of Pharisee in us can grow stronger if we are not actively seeking and getting life from a deeper relationship with God. If our life comes from knowing and loving God, then it won't matter so much whether or not the worship band plays the coolest songs and is really "tight." Our enjoyment comes primarily from loving God, not the music.

If we begin to grow cold in our love but stay in the church, we become more and more like the Pharisees. As worship leaders, we often feel pressure to look like we are growing in our relationship to God, or at least look like we are not falling away! We learn how to "keep up appearances" around our Christian friends, how to say the right things, how to look engaged during worship, even how to lead in prayer. We learn to fit in. We are tempted to hide our failures and struggles because we want those around us to think that we are a successful Christian. The pressure to belong in this way is a tremendously powerful force which we all face, until the enjoyment of God's love becomes an even greater factor, and we overcome.

In the Old Testament, the people of Israel were given a set of guidelines to follow, the Law of Moses. They failed in obeying those rules, but Jeremiah later prophesied a new day when God would place his law on our hearts.

> *Behold, the days are coming, declares the Lord, when I will make a new covenant with the house of Israel and the house of Judah, not like the covenant that I made with their fathers on the day when I took them by the hand to bring them out of the land of Egypt, my covenant that they broke, though I was their husband, declares the Lord.*
>
> *For this is the covenant that I will make with the house of Israel after those days, declares the Lord: I will put my law within them, and I will* ***write it on their hearts****. And I will be their God, and they shall be my people. – Jeremiah 31:31-33*

What does it mean to have the law of God on our hearts? God is saying that he wants us to obey because we *want* to, not because we *have* to, fearing the repercussions.

When raising children, parents usually teach by setting guidelines and giving consequences for disobeying and rewards for obedience. As we get older we begin to realize that because our parents love us and want the best for us, we would be wise to take their advice. We move past threat and rewards to obedience out of love and trust. The "law" of our parents becomes written on our hearts. We are convinced to do the right thing without needing rewards for obedience or consequences for disobedience. We have been trained.

The Pharisees in Jesus' time had become hypocrites because they obeyed God's Law outwardly, but inwardly denied his lordship.

> *You hypocrites! Well did Isaiah prophesy of you, when he said: "This people honors me with their lips, but their heart is far from me; in vain do they worship me, teaching as doctrines the commandments of men" – Matthew 15:7-9*

We can easily become as hypocritical as those Pharisees. The word hypocrisy used in the New Testament comes from the Greek word meaning an actor. An actor appears as someone they are not. Now this is fine on the stage or in a movie, but there is no place for acting in worship. Being genuine is the opposite of acting.

How can we avoid becoming a hypocrite – looking like we love Jesus, but in our hearts chasing other loves? Let's look at how we can grow even more authentic in worship . . .

7

WHEN WE DON'T FEEL LIKE IT

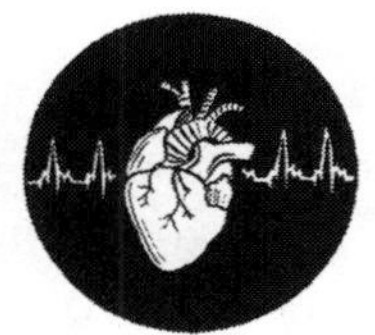

I have been asked on a number of occasions: "Aren't we being a hypocrite if we worship God when we don't feel like it?" That's a good question. It is a cry for reality, wanting our hearts and our mouths to be saying the same thing. What is the answer? How do you praise and worship God when you are going through a tough time?

One answer is that worship is a choice. So if we open our mouths and begin praising, we will often start to feel like worshiping. The point is that worship is not dependent on feelings, that we should worship God just because He is worthy of our praise.

This is generally true, and it definitely applies if we are just being lazy or if we are grumpy because we haven't had coffee yet. But it is different when we are struggling with deeply painful personal issues. I am referring to times when our hearts are discouraged, downcast or wounded by circumstances— a broken relationship, a betrayal of trust, a tragic accident, a hurtful argument with a loved one, a death in the family, or a disappointment over some failure, injustice or missed opportunity. These are not easily brushed off with a quick "Hallelujah, God is on the throne!" In these situations, we need to remind ourselves that it is a good thing to give thanks to God.

If we ignore our emotions we cheat ourselves of a major blessing. Yes, our emotions are part of the way God has made us and he has done a good job. But we've made the mistake of letting our emotions rule us at times, and so we've made some bad choices. This leads us to conclude that our emotions are unhelpful and a nuisance. Some might even say they're our enemy. However, if we see God's purpose in creating us with the capacity to feel, we can begin to deal with these emotions in a God-given way.

When I heard the phrase "emotions are the voice of our heart," I wondered if that might be a key to understanding God's purpose with our feelings. It sounded like the way physical pain works. Most of us avoid physical pain, but without it, how would we know if there was something going wrong in our body? Pain is the voice of our body. If we listen to it, we might discover what is wrong and respond. Emotions can tell us what is happening in our hearts. In Psalm 42, the writer cries out "Why are you downcast, oh my soul?" He feels emotional pain and seeks an answer to the cause.

If we come to a worship time and we are not feeling like joining in, rather than ignoring the feelings, why not ask God what is going on in your heart. He will help us see whether the source is tiredness or boredom, or something much deeper.

The Bible presents some helpful examples of dealing with emotions. They give us a clue how to get past these difficulties and into praise. In the Psalms we see David crying out to God, expressing how he felt, even if it was not with happy, victorious words. Jeremiah also complained to God about his situation. In fact, his book, Lamentations, is a cry to the Lord, a complaint, a lament.

But David and Jeremiah knew something about how to complain to God. They spoke directly to God, vocalized what they felt, but then declared what God is like. We can almost feel them receiving encouragement as we read their writings. In Lamentations 3, Jeremiah cried out to God. He even spoke of his pain as coming from God. He used intense language like "he has broken my teeth with gravel!" In fact he continues for 20 verses complaining to God, but then there's a turning, and this is the key. What he does in verses 21 onwards, is a lesson for all of us when we face difficult circumstances that dull our enthusiasm to rejoice:

> *But this I call to mind, and therefore I have hope:*
>
> *The steadfast love of the Lord never ceases; his mercies never come to an end; they are new every morning; great is your faithfulness.*
>
> *"The Lord is my portion," says my soul, "therefore I will hope in him." – Lamentations 3:21-24*

We sometimes complain to other people, hoping to extract sympathy and comfort from them. This often results in drawing them into our misery. But this is not what Jeremiah does! He complains to God first, not to his friends. Then, after he has poured out his soul, telling God exactly how he feels, he remembers what God is like, and this gives him hope for the future.

He proclaims his confidence in God's goodness, which will carry him through his trials, even in the depths of dark circumstances. He did not look to others to receive sympathy; he broke out of his misery by remembering God's mercy and faithfulness, declaring his trust in him for what is to come. That's why thanks and praise are so powerful.

In Proverbs we read that "*death and life are in the power of the tongue*" (Proverbs 18:21). We have the capacity to cultivate death or life in our situation by our words. What amazing power! In James 3 we are told how powerful our tongue is. If we could harness this power for good, our lives could be so much better. When life's treating us well, it is not hard to be positive, but when disappointments hit us, it is a lot more difficult to be upbeat. Our feelings war against it. We are tempted to lose our focus on God's ability when we become centered on our struggles.

The answer is not to disregard our feelings and "praise God anyway." If we push our feelings down and struggle to do what we believe is the "right thing," we end up suppressing the very passion that is supposed to fuel worship from our heart. If we deal with our feelings like Jeremiah and David did, we can rekindle the fire within and go even deeper in our praise and worship. But we have to do it God's way. God is looking for honest, genuine hearts. He is looking for worshipers who are the same on the inside as they proclaim to be on the outside.

As we remember what God has done in the past, and speak it out loud, faith and hope arise in us. When David was facing Goliath, I can not imagine what he was feeling inside. King Saul tries to dissuade David saying in effect: "You won't succeed... you are too young, Goliath is too experienced." (1 Samuel 17:33 paraphrased)

How did David respond? He remembered what God had done for him in the past. He told Saul how God had enabled him to defeat the lion and the bear when they threatened his sheep. Then David went further. He spoke his confidence in the future (that is, he confessed his hope). Hebrews 10:23 says,

"Hold fast to the confession of your hope without wavering, for he who promised is faithful."

Because of what God has done, and because of who God is, we can look to the future with assurance that God will always be who he says he is. When we confess this confidence with our mouth, life is released, hope returns, and the future looks brighter.

If we face up to the way we are feeling, the challenges we face, we can regain the fire by remembering who God is, and speaking it out.

In Psalm 3, David is not in a happy place! He has been betrayed by his own son, Absalom, and is fleeing for his life. So what does he want to sing about? The "man after God's own heart" knows God and what he is like. Does he "praise God anyway"? No, he pours out his heart to God; he does not hide the fact that he is in trouble. But then, like Jeremiah, he does not stay focused on his predicament. He turns to consider God's character. Verse 3 starts with "but"...

"But you, O Lord, are a shield about me, my glory, and the lifter of my head."

He is saying that although enemies are against him, God is the one who delivers, protects, encourages, and answers his cry! He goes on to say that he won't be afraid because it is God who will strike his enemies. He speaks out what God is like. That's what praise is!

This psalm is a song that David wrote and no doubt sang at that time. What an example of how to deal with our feelings! His lyrics were totally relevant to his situation; he was not happy and he said so! We need to make sure our songs today speak with similar honesty and openness?

In his darkest moments, David even resorted to saying things that were not even true, in a literal sense. In Psalm 142, David is pictured hiding from Saul's army in a cave. He could not have been happy, I know I wouldn't be if 3,000 soldiers were chasing me and trying to kill me! His painful song includes these words in verse 4: *"There is none who takes notice of me . . . no one cares for my soul."* Was this true? I am sure he had friends who cared for him; why else would they have followed him so loyally? So while this statement is probably not literally true, it is a true statement about his feelings. I think it is okay to express exactly how we feel, even if our words are not literally true, as long as we follow David's example of how to follow up these expressions. He cried out to God for deliverance and affirmed God's care for him. Right after complaining that no one cared, he said, "You are my refuge."

Let's go past "praise God anyway," and begin to express our feelings to God, being careful to follow with thanks, praise, and "confessions of our hope."

When we are feeling lonely, we can declare: "Lord, I'm lonely, but you are here, and you are my comfort." When people have let us down, we can cry out: "Lord, my friends have stabbed me in the back, but you are faithful and will always be kind and loving." No matter what we are going through, God is able to rescue us. When we know his character, we are able to describe to him what is happening to us and then counter with the "but, you are..."

In Proverbs 4:23 (NASB) we are warned to *"Watch over your heart with all diligence, For from it flow the springs of life."*

Thanks and praise that blesses God

Our worship can lose its effectiveness either by being too me-centered or by denying our feelings. If we have managed to express our heart to God and have received his encouragement, it helps if we consider how our thanks and praise affects God. Worship works so much better when we think about both our feelings and God's feelings. When I pondered the words in Song of Songs 4:9 I began to imagine how God might feel when we praise him.

> *"you have captivated my heart, my sister, my bride, you have captivated my heart with one glance of your eyes . . ."*

The Hebrew word for captivated literally means "to make the heart beat faster." Could my praise have an effect on God's heart? When I teach on worship, I get members of the class to thank or praise one another to illustrate both their understanding of the topic and the effect our words have on the way we feel. It is delightful to see the smiles on both the giver and the receiver of affirmation. The motives of the ones offering praise are usually unselfish love. They truly are looking to bless the person, not themselves. If our motive is to bless God and not to please ourselves, it pleases God, and because he loves us so much, he wants to bless us in return. It can change the way we feel in worship as we imagine God smiling at us.

So we must check our hearts before entering in, but then offer to God thanks and praise as we realize how much it is blessing him. So it is not all about us or all about God. It is both. It is a two-way flow of love and respect in a relationship.

PART II

A ROAD MAP TO GUIDE US

8

WHAT ARE WE SINGING ABOUT?

It is interesting to note that the largest book in the Bible is the Psalms, the book of song lyrics. We haven't been given the music to these songs, which suggests to me that God is more interested in the thoughts expressed in the words than the music we choose as accompaniment. Music will be different all over the world, in different age groups and different denominations, but the truths in the lyrics must be firmly rooted in God's unchanging Word, no matter what the cultural container.

Why songs?

When so many are saying that "worship is more than singing songs," we can lose sight of why we sing at all. Singing is by far the most mentioned mode of thanksgiving and praise in the Bible. It becomes so "normal' to us that its value can be lost, and songs can be downplayed as not important.

Songs are a powerful way to express our love, especially when we gather. Firstly, songs enable us to bring all our voices together to say the same thing, unified confessions of thanks and praise. The rhythm and meter of each song helps us to keep together. If you have ever tried to get a group of people to recite something unfamiliar without music, you'll know that's so much more difficult than teaching a new song.

Secondly, melodies can add emotional strength to our statements about God. Songs also help us to remember timeless truths. Most of us can remember songs we learned in our childhood, and the thoughts in those lyrics stay with us for many years. The teaching ability of songs is so powerful!

So singing is perhaps the primary way to praise God. The other biblical expressions, such as dancing, clapping, and raising hands, are dwarfed in comparison to the Bible's emphasis on singing.

What are we singing about?

True worship is a combination of an inward motive and an outward action. Part of our worship experience should be a pursuit of truth.

It is easy to lose contact with the lyrics when we are singing, and just enjoy the feeling of worship and closeness to God. While that still blesses us and God, it is dangerous to ignore the truths expressed in the songs. It is entirely possible to get lost in the music and fun of our gatherings and lose connection to God.

What we are left with is feelings-based worship, which is not all bad, but the truth should stir our hearts more than the music. If the enjoyment of the songs is solely based on the music, then could it really be called worship? **Our hearts must**

connect with the truth of the lyrics if singing is to have value in the spirit realm.

This does not mean we always have to be singing words that our minds comprehend. There are times when our voices cry out from the depths of our hearts with sounds that don't have to make sense to our minds. There are times when we might just sing a wordless melody, "oo-oo-ooh" or "la-la-la." Another time to have our minds bypassed is when singing in the spirit, that is, in tongues. Paul urges us in 1 Corinthians 14 to not only sing with our understanding but also in the spirit, in a language we don't understand in our minds. But when we are singing in our own language, with our understanding, we need to know what the words say! The Psalms use words of truth, and so must we.

There is amazing spiritual power in personally and corporately declaring the truth. We are bombarded constantly with lies from the enemy and the truth sets us free from these lies. Missing this is like going to war, and leaving behind the weapons God has given us. We have seen how King David knew how to use truths about God's character to counter the lies he encountered daily. We see that in his Psalms, which were written as lyrics to be sung.

Learning the language - communicating with God

Often today we use the word worship to include everything that happens when a worship team plays songs. If we sing it in a congregation, we call it a worship song. An album with songs about God is usually called a "worship album." We have bundled all our different thoughts and feelings and types of communication to God into just one word, "worship." We used to use the term "praise and worship" when I was younger. Of course, the big question being asked then was: "what is the difference between praise and worship?" I don't hear that question being asked as much now, probably because now it is all called worship.

Distinguishing between praise and worship was a challenge that led me on a journey of discovery through the Bible.

Where are we going?

What was I doing when I led "praise and worship?" What was I trying to get people to do when I led these songs? I had to know what I was doing, where I was going.

A friend was traveling from my hometown, Kona, to Honolulu. He boarded a plane at our little airport, and as he did, two planes were boarding at the same time. We don't have jetways like most other airports, we walk across the tarmac and climb the stairs. As he sat in his seat (they were unassigned at that time), he was welcomed onto the flight to Maui! He had boarded the wrong flight! Fortunately, he was able to get off before the plane started taxiing. It pays to know where you are going, and how to get there, or you might end up in the wrong place!

What are we trying to do? How do we get there? My journey began as I was drawn to contemplate Psalm 100:4:

"Enter his gates with thanksgiving and his courts with praise"

I was discovering that moving towards the presence of God required thanks and praise. Psalm 100:4 starts with thanksgiving, then moves to praise. I felt God was directing me to not only know where we were going, but how to get there. What were the keys? Thanks, praise and worship. What did these three mean?

Let's look deeper . . . .

9

THANKSGIVING

As I approached the microphone and the sea of faces before me, I inwardly expressed my heart to God. "Thank you Lord for dying on the cross for me. I have been saved by your grace. Thank you!" Once again, I needed to be in the right frame of mind to lead a larger group in worship. Successfully leading a congregation in exuberant praise is "heady wine," when the band is "in the groove" and everyone is right into it. As worship leaders, we are tempted to become intoxicated with our own success, as it "goes to our head" and becomes pride.

It is easy to accept the glory for ourselves for what God is doing, to feel that it is our talents that make meetings go so well. A pastor friend gave me a sound word of advice when he saw God using me to lead others in worship. He said, "Stay close to the message of the cross." So, many times when I was tempted to fall into the pride trap, I would thank God for salvation as I began to lead worship.

As I continued to thank God in everyday life, I began to understand its importance in praise and worship.

What does Psalm 100:4 suggest to us about thanksgiving,

gates, and entering God's presence? Gates are an entry point. They keep the wrong people out and let the right people in.

I remember going to Progressive Field, the home field of the Cleveland Indians baseball team. As I lined up outside the gate, I could see thousands of people inside the stadium. I love the thrill of being in a packed stadium, hearing the crowd cheer, enjoying two teams locked in battle! As I approached the gate, I was confident that I would soon be seated. Why? Because I held something that qualified me for entrance to the stadium. It was a ticket for that particular game on that very day. The attendant looked at my ticket and allowed me through the gates. I was in.

What qualifies us to enter the presence of a king? There are special procedures we must learn if we are to meet a king or queen. What about the King of kings? We enter his gates with thanksgiving. I wondered what thanksgiving had to do with qualifying.

We read in the book of Hebrews that we can enter God's presence because of what Jesus did for us on the cross.

> *"Therefore, brothers, since we have confidence to enter the holy places by the blood of Jesus, by the new and living way that he opened for us through the curtain . . . " – Hebrews 10:19-20*

In the Old Testament, the High Priest in Israel was allowed to enter the Holy of Holies, just once a year, and only after sprinkling blood of the sin offering. Our Great High Priest Jesus died in our place, a once-and-for-all sacrifice for sin. Now we don't have to kill bulls and sheep to make it possible to be in his presence. And better yet, we can approach him anytime.

Jesus taught us to remember his death and resurrection by talking about bread and wine at the passover meal. He wanted us to continually give thanks for his sacrifice on the cross. We remember, and give thanks for what he has done. Our attitude toward the cross has much to do with experiencing his presence.

In Psalm 24:3 David asks "who qualifies to be in God's presence?"

> *"Who shall ascend the hill of the LORD? And who shall stand in his holy place?"*

It is the ones who have clean hands and a pure heart. We are cleansed from sin and have our hearts changed by trusting in God's forgiveness. We can "stand in the holy place" because Jesus paid the price for us.

I began to see the importance of our heart attitude if we want to see the King. It was part of the protocol, the correct way to approach him. We can't approach Jesus with pride in our heart. In a larger group, in corporate worship, we must gather together in humility, but with confidence in Jesus's sacrifice. That's the way to enter God's courts. The presence of God in a church meeting is different from the way he is with us personally throughout our lives. To experience and feel his touch has been my goal in leading others in worship. For me, it has always begun with my own thankfulness for the cross.

In Deuteronomy 8, Moses urged the people of Israel to give thanks to God when they became prosperous in the promised land. He warned that if they did not thank God, then their hearts would be lifted up in pride and take the credit for their success.

We enter his gates by thanking Jesus for what he has done for us on the cross. Through thanks and humility we qualify to enter. Only the cleansed and forgiven can live in the presence of such a holy God. He does not receive us because we are mature or our singing sounds great, he welcomes the humble who trust in his forgiveness and acceptance. He welcomes us into his presence even though we may be weak and fail occasionally. God's incredible grace allows us to "enter boldly into the throne room" (Hebrews 10:19).

Worship leaders must continually remember that God's enjoyment of our worship does not depend on how our songs sound. I don't think God is impressed with our music. He is the inventor of music after all. A father is not usually impressed with the technical skill of his three-year-old daughter when she paints a picture for him. He is impressed with her heart of love. So it is with our songs. It is not the brilliance of our musicianship or the eloquence of our words that God accepts. He looks at our hearts to see who he lets through the gates into his presence. He detests fake worship (Isaiah 29:13) no matter how good it sounds.

Thanking God involves both remembrance and proclamation. There is great power in recalling what God has done and speaking it out. Proverbs 18:21 reminds us, *"Death and life are in the power of the tongue."*

The children of Israel often forgot what God had done (Psalm 77). I find it amazing that they would forget miracles like the Red Sea parting, but they did. We can be just like that; we easily forget what God has done in our lives and in those around us. He wants us to both remember his good works, and to vocalize them.

Remembering God's goodness and speaking out our appreciation has many rewards. Thanks gives us hope for the future, strengthens our faith and guards against unbelief.

I was part of a YWAM outreach from our Holmsted base in

England, to Venice, Italy, when I was faced with a challenge. After our month on the streets sharing God's love, I was invited to travel to Denmark with YWAM friends. Afterward I would need to find a way to get back to England. It sounded like fun, but I had been learning not to rely on my own thinking. I needed to pray and see if it was something that God was blessing. I went away and prayed and felt God was allowing me to go.

One reason they asked me was the need to fill their van with paying passengers! I did not have the money to go with them or to get back to England, so I prayed a prayer often repeated while serving with YWAM. "Lord, I feel you are leading me to do this, now, will you please provide for me." The very next day I received a check from New Zealand, which was quite unexpected. I cashed the check and told the friends I could travel with them.

The next day we left, traveling through Europe. After the time in Denmark, I arrived in London on an overnight ferry and found my way to Victoria Station to catch the train back to the base at Holmsted Manor, West Sussex. I remembered how far I had traveled on the proceeds of that check. My heart was full of gratitude. That check arrived the day after I had prayed, and the day before the van left for Denmark. Could there have been a more precise timing for God's provision? One day earlier and it wouldn't have been an answer to prayer, one day later and I wouldn't have been able to make the trip. Was that just good luck, a coincidence? No, for me it was one more example of God's faithfulness and goodness.

Many times since then I have remembered that story and told it to others. Now, even as I write I am remembering God's faithfulness during that time. It gives me courage and hope to keep believing him for the provision to do his will.

A few years ago we had an opportunity to buy a home. My wife, Liz, and I had often dreamed of owning our own but an opportunity had not arisen. Until then! When we were confronted with a deadline to make the final decision to buy, we still had not received enough for the deposit. We gained courage by remembering God's provision over many years. We heard God's clear "yes," made the decision, and within two weeks we had the full deposit. God is good! The stories we tell unfold a convincing picture of God's faithfulness to provide.

If we forget what God has done we can lapse into unbelief when we encounter challenges in our walk with God. When we give thanks we are built up in our faith because we are concentrating on God's ability not our own. When we remember how God has provided for us in the past, and thank him, we gain confidence in the future and courage to act. We are encouraged to believe he can and will do it again!

Thanksgiving for the cross opens us to the presence of God in worship. Thanksgiving for God's past guidance and provision encourages us to trust and proclaim God's faithfulness to ourselves and others. And it leads to a awareness of his character that gets expressed in praise. But what is praise? Let's find out!

10
PRAISE

In normal life, we praise all kinds of things. We praise movies; we praise food; we praise computers. We praise cars, clothes, cell phones, gardens, houses, so many things. We praise people. What do we say when we praise someone? Let's say we have a friend named Jim and we'd like to commend him to a future employer. We consider Jim's good qualities and express them verbally. We tell of his diligence, dependability, his skill and creativity. We might even give some examples. We are praising Jim. Would we say "praise Jim, oh praise Jim?" No, that sounds weird. It might also sound strange to some when worship leaders repeat aloud, "Praise Jesus. Praise you Lord."

I was worshiping with a group of young people on a beach mission on Australia's Sunshine Coast. We would begin each day gathering under a large tent, singing praises to God, praying for his direction, and listening to teaching. As we sang, one of my friends kept shouting "Hallelujah! Praise you Lord! Glory to God!" over and over. I listened and wondered if this was some special Bible language I must use.

That set me on a journey to discover more of the meaning of

praise. I searched through the Bible, dictionaries, concordances and lexicons. I looked up English words, I looked up Greek and Hebrew words, I looked at every verse in the Bible that mentioned worship or praise. Even though I had become familiar with new musical styles and new forms of worship in the church, I still did not truly understand what praise was and whether it was different from worship.

I asked God to give me revelation as I studied, and he answered my prayer. It is one of the joys of life when an idea comes and you know it must be God because it explains so much, and it just makes sense. I had the answer I was looking for. I was beginning to understand Bible praise!

Psalm 100:4 continues, "and into his courts with praise." When we have entered his gates with thanksgiving, we can see the beauty of the One we adore, the One who has saved us and loves us. We instantly recognize he deserves all the praise we can give. We praise his many great attributes, and as we do, we become even more aware of his greatness, his mercy and his love.

The Hebrew word used most often for praise is *halal*. I noticed it is used in the Bible the same way as our English word praise. To praise someone is simply to speak out their good qualities. I pondered this thought for a while and the lights came on! It might not seem very profound at first, but this idea revolutionized the way I express myself to God. I began seeing what the Bible meant when it says repeatedly: "Praise the Lord!"

As I searched God's Word, I now found expressive, creative language of praise in the Psalms, especially Psalm 145. The title for this psalm in the original Hebrew text is "A Psalm of Praise." It is the only psalm with a title like this. I figured that a title like that might help me understand praise. I looked at the content, and it is full of declaring what God is like. After a couple of verses of introduction, David launches into speaking out the character qualities of God, verse after verse. Here are some of my favorites:

> *The Lord upholds all who are falling and raises up all who are bowed down.*
>
> *The eyes of all look to you, and you give them their food in due season.*
>
> *You open your hand; you satisfy the desire of every living thing.*
>
> *The Lord is righteous in all his ways and kind in all his works.*
>
> *The Lord is near to all who call on him, to all who call on him in truth.*
>
> *He fulfills the desire of those who fear him; he also hears their cry and saves them. – Psalm 145:14-19*

David says what God is like, that's praise, speaking out God's wonderful attributes.

In the New Testament, we find a statement in the book of Hebrews about praise.

> *"Through him then let us continually offer up a sacrifice of praise to God, that is, the fruit of lips that acknowledge his name." – Hebrews 13:15*

What is meant by the phrase "fruit of lips that acknowledge his name?" Does it mean that praise is saying "Jesus, Jesus," over and over, like a literal English interpretation might suggest? The Greek word translated as "acknowledge" is *homologeo* which means "to speak the same as, to confess." I also looked at what might be meant by the word "name." In Hebrew culture, name means more than just a label, it might include your character, reputation or position in society. So to say "acknowledge his name" likely means "to speak in agreement of what God is like, his character and reputation." It seems this verse is saying that praise is speaking out what God is like. This is how we use the word *praise* in English. It just makes sense!

As I listened to others repeating "praise the Lord," it occurred to me that this biblical phrase was one spoken not to God, but to one another. We are encouraging one another to praise the Lord. The words really mean "come on, let us praise, let us open our mouths and say what God is like."

The statement "Praise the Lord" is not really praise in that sense, it does not say what God is like. It is simply an encouragement to praise. Saying "let's eat" is not eating, saying "let's go shopping" is not shopping.

It may appear that we are just getting fussy with words. You could say that, but most of our conversation depends on us using words that others understand. Speaking phrases that don't mean what we are saying is not good communication. It is a recipe for confusion. Words are important. Words are powerful. If we don't understand the words we are using, are we really communicating? Often our praise is merely imagining nice thoughts about God, and then repeating popular religious phrases, whether they make any sense or not.

As I continued to participate in praise and worship times, I found myself struggling to reconcile these new thoughts about praise with what was going on around me. "How can I praise God? I don't know what to say!" So I thought I would develop a language of praise by letting the Bible teach me. I read through God's songbook, the book of Psalms, I used my purple-colored pencil to mark the passages that spoke of God's character. When others around me would be crying out "Hallelujah, praise the Lord," I would open my Bible and read the passages I had colored. Sure, it was awkward, but something happened in my relationship with God. My mind began to be filled with knowledge of what he is like as I began to learn a new language of praise.

As our minds ponder God's character and our mouths speak it out, our hearts are drawn to experience his presence. As the truth of God's love fills us, we are encouraged and strengthened. It is uplifting to speak out how God loves us, cares for us, provides, protects and defends us.

I am not trying to ban the use of certain phrases. I am wanting to help us express our hearts in meaningful language that will not only bless God, but us and others also. If we want to be intentional about praising God, we have to understand what praise is.

There's a popular phrase in the church that I still love to hear. "God is good, all the time, all the time, God is good." That's praise! It says He is good and He is faithful. As we repeat those words, we are reminded of God's goodness, even when we struggle, even when we are having a bad day, in loss or disappointment. Our confession of God's goodness has power to keep us from discouragement. Speaking out about God's love helps us feel loved. Proclaiming God's faithfulness to his promises helps us believe his word to us.

The power of praise originates from affirming all that he is, it is not in singing heartily. The effectiveness of our praise is not in how loud we sing, but how much our hearts are meaning what we say, and saying what we mean, concerning who God is and what He is like.

Colossians 3:16 instructs us to let God's word be rich as we sing:

> *"Let the word of Christ dwell in you richly, teaching and admonishing one another in all wisdom, singing psalms and hymns and spiritual songs, with thankfulness in your hearts to God."*

Let's learn a rich language of praise that's powerful because it is full of meaning, expressing truth. Let's move past the exhortations to praise, "Hallelujah", and "Praise the Lord" and begin to praise God like David did in Psalm 145.

As we linger in his courts with praise, we become aware of the arresting presence of the merciful, loving, compassionate King who is also the majestic, powerful Creator of the universe. What is our response? We begin to worship . . .

11

WORSHIP

"Oh come, let us worship and bow down; Let us kneel before the LORD our Maker;" (Psalm 95:6)

"The king has brought me into his chambers." (Song of Songs 1:4)

"God is Spirit, and those who worship him must worship in spirit and truth." (John 4:24)

W***hat is Worship?*** Sometimes when we use the word *worship,* we are meaning different things. Sometimes we refer to the whole church service, including singing, prayers, offering, announcements and the sermon, it is all called worship in this sense.

Often we mean just the singing part of the service. For years, churches used the term, "praise and worship," but now it is more common to just say, *worship*. We have worship leaders, worship teams, worship recordings, and worship conferences, all dealing with Christian singing. When we use the word worship this way, our words reinforce the idea that worship is singing songs. But anyone who has read through the Bible knows that worship is more than songs, So what then is it?

Confusion often comes when we use the word to define the whole church service while other times referring to the singing part of the service as worship. I have heard pastors say, "Wasn't that a wonderful time of worship!" and "thank you worship team." Then in the next breath say, "We are going to continue our worship by giving our offerings or hearing the preacher." So, if I am the worship leader at that place, I am wondering: "What did I just lead? Was it just songs?" If the whole church service was worship, what was the "worship time" about? Or is it all worship? So we are left wondering what is truly worship!

To add even more fuzziness, more Christian leaders have been using the word worship to describe the attitude of giving God honor in all aspects of our lives. Rather than speaking of worship as an activity, it has become just an attitude. Of course, everything we do should be done to honor God, but is this what the Bible calls worship? I fear we are losing the Bible meaning of worship, because we have not taken care to see what the Bible teaches.

When the Bible uses the Hebrew word *shachah* and the Greek word *proskuneo,* it always refers to a specific action, not merely an attitude of heart. When people worshiped in the Bible, they were not doing anything else. We see the same in both the Old and New Testaments. Worship was a separate, focused time, often spontaneous. Praise was a more organized activity. King David commanded the Levites to praise at specific, regular times, planned into their schedule!

Praise acknowledges and expresses who God is; worship responds to who he is by expressing our commitment to him, our allegiance, our honor and love.

Praise says "He is Lord." Worship says "You are my Lord."

Praise says "God is love." Worship says "I love you!"

Praise says "God is faithful." Worship says "I will follow you always"

Praise says "God is awesome." Worship does not say anything, we just fall on our faces!

In praise, we remind ourselves of God's love for us. In worship we respond to that knowledge by allowing ourselves to be embraced by that love, letting it soak further into our hearts! Worship is the place of deeper heart connection with God, expressing the inner-most thoughts and feelings.

In our earthly relationships, we may talk about everyday things like, "What shall we eat today?" or "Please take out the trash." We can talk to God about everyday things too, but there are times when we must talk about issues closer to our hearts.

When I began dating Liz, we talked about all kinds of things. When I wanted to take our relationship further than "just friends," I stumbled over my words, but that didn't matter. I just took a deep breath, and shared honestly from my heart. It was a special time. Our relationship began. Months later, I asked her the big question, "Will you marry me?" Her simple words, "Yes, I will," took us to an even deeper place. We had expressed our love, and committed to a life together. We were changed! It was not an ordinary time, it was precious, one to be remembered for a long time.

We live most of our lives in the ordinary, that's OK. But it would not be very exciting if all our life was like that. We love special times like Christmas and birthdays. Married couples enjoy date nights. We have special days, special clothes, special songs, and special places to visit. Our life of serving God involves lots of ordinary, mundane activities. If we love and serve God, then every activity is for God, a life lived for his glory. Worship is a part of that life, lived for God's glory, but it is unique, it is separate from the ordinary. It is a time to be especially close to God. It can be anywhere, at any time; it does not have to be in church or in meetings. But it is unlike other activities! Expressing issues of the heart with our close friends requires the right time, the right place, and the right atmosphere. Worship is like that too.

One time when I was teaching a class on worship, I wondered whether all my brilliant biblical explanations and reasoning were really helping the students understand. I paused, and exclaimed, "I think you all know what worship is, it is this!" I looked up to heaven, closed my eyes and raised my hands, but said nothing. I was acting, but they nodded in agreement. "Yeah, we know what you mean!" It does not have to look like that, with closed eyes, or hands raised, but the students in that class recognized what I was communicating to God by my posture. They got it!

Thanksgiving expresses our appreciation for what God has done, and praise says what God is like. Worship takes us further than both thanks and praise. As his amazing love probes deeper into our hearts, and as a revelation of his greatness begins to shatter our too-small perspective on God, we commune with him face to face.

We respond to his presence in whatever way is appropriate. He is King, he is Father, he is the Bridegroom. We express to our King our allegiance, our dedication to his will. We don't say this lightly. We may also convey our deep respect and love for our heavenly Father. This is worship; communicating deep things during a special time. We put down our tools, our daily work, and concentrate on him alone.

It is exclusive, it is intense, it is focused attention that draws from us precious thoughts and feelings towards our God. It may or may not involve music. It can be sung, spoken, demonstrated with our bodies by bowing or kneeling or even in silence as we stand in awe. The method is not important, but it must involve communicating honestly.

Worship conveys the yearnings of our innermost being, from the core of who we are. That's why it is so powerful and life-changing. It is deep. It takes our relationship with God further, because we have spent quality time, intimate time that refreshes us. When we are in his presence like this our cares and concerns fade, our discouragement disappears, our wounds are soothed, our need for love is met, and we are strengthened to serve.

But isn't worship a lifestyle?

When I first heard people speak of worship as a lifestyle, I was a bit confused. If it meant that we should offer God praise and worship at any time during the week, and not just on Sundays, then I agreed. If it suggested that every part of our lives must be lived for God and for his glory, then I would certainly agree.

But did a lifestyle of worship mean everything we did was worship? I began to chew on it. If all of life was worship, then what was worship? In all honesty, many things we do during the week are more self-focused than God-focused. There is often a mismatch between how we sing on Sunday in church and how we act on Monday. We are encouraged to change this, to live our lives in a sacrificial, worshipful way. I applaud any efforts to do so. But does saying it is all worship achieve the desired change? I doubt it.

We could also say that the way we live our lives demonstrates the gospel, and therefore our whole lives are evangelism. St. Francis is quoted as saying, "Preach the gospel at all times and if necessary use words." That appears to be very wise, but looking deeper, that kind of thinking will ultimately lead to a de-emphasis on preaching. Ideas have consequences. We certainly want to live godly lives that draw people to Christ, but if we don't use our words to tell them about Jesus, I doubt we have really evangelized.

So the wrestling with these ideas continued. If everything was worship, then what was I leading people to do in our "praise and worship" times? Was there any content or meaning in the word "worship" that would help me know what I was doing as a worship leader? The answer had to be found in the Bible, so I began searching.

As I combed the Bible from Genesis to Revelation, I found that when people worshiped, they were usually encountering God in a different way from their normal lives. These groups or individuals worshiped in a variety of places, by bowing, kneeling, and sometimes even standing. They were often not in the temple. David worshiped on top of a hill, others where they were standing at the time. They worshiped in response to different circumstances: hearing God speak, feeling his presence, or going through a rough time.

Here's some examples . .

INDIVIDUALS WORSHIPED AT SPECIFIC TIMES PROMPTED BY SPECIFIC CIRCUMSTANCES . . .

- **Jacob** – *"By faith Jacob, when dying, blessed each of the sons of Joseph, bowing in worship over the head of his staff" (Hebrews 11:21)*
- **Moses** *"bowed his head toward the earth and worshiped." (Exodus 34:8)*
- **David** *"arose from the earth and washed and anointed himself and*

changed his clothes. And he went into the house of the Lord and worshiped. He then went to his own house. And when he asked, they set food before him, and he ate." (2 Samuel 12:20).

• **Gideon** - *"As soon as Gideon heard the telling of the dream and its interpretation, he worshiped. And he returned to the camp of Israel and said, "Arise, for the Lord has given the host of Midian into your hand." (Judges 7:15).*

• **Job** - *"Then Job arose and tore his robe and shaved his head and fell on the ground and worshiped." (Job 1:20).*

• **Joshua** *" fell on his face to the earth and worshiped, and said to him, "What does my lord say to his servant?" (Joshua 5:14)*

• **Hannah** - *"They rose early in the morning and worshiped before the Lord; then they went back to their house at Ramah." (1Samuel 1:19)*

• **Jehoshaphat** *"bowed his head with his face to the ground, and all Judah and the inhabitants of Jerusalem fell down before the Lord, worshiping the Lord." (2Chronicles 20:18).*

• **Paul** - *"You can verify that it is not more than twelve days since I went up to worship in Jerusalem"* (Acts 24:11)

GROUPS ALSO WORSHIPED AT SPECIFIC TIMES...

• **The children of Israel** - *"And the people believed; and when they heard that the Lord had visited the people of Israel and that he had seen their affliction, they bowed their heads and worshiped." (Exodus 4:31, also Exodus 33:10, 2 Chronicles 7:3, 29:28),*

• **Hezekiah and all the people** - *"When the offering was finished, the king and all who were present with him bowed themselves and worshiped." (2 Chronicles 29:29)*

• **The Wise Men** - *"And going into the house they saw the child with Mary his mother, and they fell down and worshiped him." (Matthew 2:11)*

• **The disciples in the boat** - *And those in the boat worshiped him, saying, "Truly you are the Son of God." (Matthew 14:33)*

• **The twenty-four elders** *"fall down before him who is seated on the throne and worship him who lives forever and ever..." (Revelation 4:10).*

• **The angels** - *"And all the angels were standing around the throne and around the elders and the four living creatures, and they fell on their faces before the throne and worshiped God" (Revelation 7:11)*

FROM THESE EXAMPLES we see that worship was a special event in people's lives. What was being communicated? Was there anything different from the rest of life? Yes, there was!

When these people worshiped God, they expressed their hearts in a number of ways. I observed that worship was a separate action sharing specific ideas, thoughts or attitudes. The word "worship" referred to the action of revealing these thoughts. Worship involved a special encounter with God that prompted them to express their hearts in a deeper and more intimate way than usual.

So what meaning is contained in the Bible words, *shachah* and *proskuneo*? What does the Bible say about worship? In the Bible, these words mean bowing or prostrating to communicate honor, respect, allegiance, submission, or love, to honor someone higher than ourselves, like a king, or God himself.

The Bible doesn't restrict worship to any particular method of expression, or any usual place or time. The most common instruction about worship is the warning not to worship idols, but to worship God alone. But the above examples demonstrate that Bible worship contains elements that distinguish it from other activities. There is usually a special meeting with God, a heart moved in some way, and a response in giving honor, an expression of submission, allegiance or love, or acts of dedication.

There is nothing so awesome, so life-giving as to experience the tangible presence of God's love. When our hearts are bowed in humility and our voices speak of his wonderful qualities, we can "enter his gates with thanksgiving and into his courts with praise." What a privilege! When we focus our hearts on God like this, the Holy Spirit is able to comfort, strengthen and encourage us as we enjoy the presence of the King of kings! Thanksgiving and praise open the door. Let's walk through that entrance into his sweet presence in worship!

> *"You make known to me the path of life; in your presence there is fullness of joy; at your right hand are pleasures forevermore." – Psalm 16:11*

12

LOVE AND RESPECT

What heart attitudes please God when we approach him in worship? Two stand out. Love and respect.

I was once asked to teach on the subject of "The Fear of the Lord." I hadn't done that before so I launched into some serious study.

One of my discoveries was that the New Testament word for fear, *phobos,* is used in two distinct ways. Not only for a sense of terror or fright, but also as deep awe and respect.

It occurred to me that in worship "the fear of the Lord" did not mean we are to be terrified or frightened of God, but rather we need to have a deep sense of awe in his presence.

Walking into one of the great cathedrals in Europe can provoke in us that sense of awe as we see the grandeur and beauty of these architectural declarations of God's glory. For some of us, we have sensed the same but in different settings such as getting our first glance of a majestic mountain range.

But when we read about the fear of the Lord, it is difficult to avoid the common use of the word fear, meaning anticipation of harm. Should we be frightened of God? Surely not! So what could it mean to walk in the fear of the Lord?

Recently I heard an illustration that helped me understand it more clearly. It was said that the fear of the Lord could be compared to our attitude to electricity. We don't live in fear of electricity thinking that any moment we could suffer harm. But we do respect it and make sure we don't misuse it or break commonly understood guidelines of its use. We don't go poking metal knives into a toaster or wall sockets. We teach our children of the dangers and protect them by covering electrical outlets. Electricity is a powerful force that enriches our lives but could prove fatal if mishandled.

In a similar way, we should respect the awesome power and complete holiness of God. If we fail to follow his guidelines we could suffer eternal consequences - even worse than death itself. He is worthy of our deepest respect.

When people in the Bible encountered the holy presence of God, they usually fell down in worship, expressing awe and respect by bowing or prostrating. We could say, then, that the fear of the Lord is an attitude of worship.

But there is another heart attitude that must be present as we worship. It is love. To meet God is to encounter love because God is love. Jesus summed up the entire law by saying that we must love God as our first priority. It shows us that loving God and being loved is extremely important and foundational to our relationship.

In the Book of Ephesians, Paul commands husbands to love their wives as Christ loved the church and that wives should respect their husbands. So we see God mentioning marriage as an analogy of Christ loving the church, and it is characterized by these two aspects, love and respect.

I was intrigued by an illustration used by British Bible teacher, David Pawson. He saw the relationship between Prince William and Kate Middleton as a picture, in a small way, of our connection with God. Kate came into the marriage because of her love for Prince William, but her respect had to go beyond that given to a normal husband. She was entering the British Royal Family and had to respect her husband as the future King of England. Love and respect together.

In worship, these two attitudes are required to adequately honor God. Love manifests as warmth, tenderness, emotion or excitement; but respect expresses submission, homage, honor, awe and reverence. If we express an awesome respect without love, we might reflect a cold or distant God. But, on the other hand, if we love God without this deep respect, we miss important aspects of his character: greatness, power and holiness. He is both a loving God and a holy God and therefore is worthy of both our love and respect.

13

THINKERS AND FEELERS

"Some people are thinkers and some are feelers." Everything within me shouted "Noooooo, don't say that." I was listening to one of the classes at our Kona campus, and I wrestled with the idea that we could be classified in such a way. It was too easy to assume that thinkers were inferior at feeling and feelers lacked the ability to think. In Western society, thinkers have often been considered more advanced and superior. Feelers have been regarded as less intelligent and subject to unhelpful mood swings.

Most Christians today acknowledge that God feels. However, because classical theology has taught that God is unaffected in his feelings, this view continues to influence Christian world view. I notice this whenever I mention "feeling the presence of God" in worship. I am confronted with the idea that worship is not about feelings, but about the truth. Now this is partly true, worship is about truth, but if God's truth does not affect our feelings, then we are missing out on one of the most satisfying benefits of worship, feeling God's love. Not just believing it, not just confessing it, but actually feeling it! If we never feel God's love, can we truly say we have a relationship with him? Yes, there are times when we have to hang on to the truth when we don't feel it. But if that's all we ever experience then we are missing out big time!

God has endowed us with the ability to think and feel and both need to be active and alive when connecting to God in worship. God's truth, when it touches beyond our minds into our hearts, will trigger godly emotions of love and acceptance. Truth does not have to remain in our minds, we need to allow it into the depths of our being, our heart. It is the Holy Spirit that takes the words of truth, from our heads, as we speak his praise, and lights up our hearts to feel God's love.

God's gift is abundant life, life that bubbles up from within as John mentions in John 7 - "out of his innermost being, rivers of living water flow."

Two verses in Paul's letters that mention singing to God give additional insight.

> *"Let the word of Christ dwell in you richly, teaching and admonishing one another in all wisdom, singing psalms and hymns and spiritual songs, with thankfulness in your hearts to God." – Colossians 3: 16*

It speaks of content and meaning when it says "let the word of Christ dwell in you richly" as you sing. A passage in Ephesians talks about being filled with the Spirit as we sing. We not only need content, but feeling as well.

> *"And do not get drunk with wine, for that is debauchery, but be filled with the Spirit, addressing one another in psalms and hymns and spiritual songs, singing and making melody to the Lord with your heart" – Ephesians 5:18-19*

In this verse, being filled with the Spirit of God is being compared to drunkenness. We see the same comparison in Acts 2 when the Holy Spirit fell at Pentecost. Some thought their strange behavior must be the effects of new wine! Peter explained that they were not drunk, but filled with the Spirit which the prophet Joel had foretold.

So how were these disciples acting to prompt such a response like this?

For them to be mocked for being drunk they must have looked like being drunk. Sometimes God's Spirit comes on people in unusual ways, and when this happens, emotions are involved. Pentecost was obviously an extreme case, but God's presence still touches people today in a variety of ways involving both thoughts and feelings, minds and emotions.

Noted British evangelical, Martin Lloyd Jones, in his book "Revival" says:

> *"we must never forget that the Holy Spirit affects the whole person . . . . man is body, soul, and spirit, and you cannot divide these. And anything which comes powerfully to any part of man is liable to affect the other parts of men. . . . Man reacts as a whole. And it is just folly to expect that he can react in the realm of the spiritual without anything at all happening to the rest of him, to the soul, and to the body."*

As we sing, let us use our God-given minds and our redeemed emotions to fully enjoy the presence of God in our praise and worship.

14

WHAT IF WE DON'T LIKE THE MUSIC?

God has BIG EARS! That phrase came to me as I was teaching in a church that was wrestling with change. We all have music that we prefer, and often the pleasure we gain in worship stems from our enjoyment of the music. So what happens when the musicians in our church play music we don't like? Shall we sit respectfully silent or join in?

Our ears are very small, but God's are big. He can listen to any kind of music we sing, and I am confident he delights in many kinds of music. Remember he is looking at our hearts, and he is not bothered by what style he is hearing.

In Isaiah 55:9 the Lord declares, *"As the heavens are higher than the earth, so are my ways higher than your ways and my thoughts than your thoughts."*

If we can accept that God is blessed by our genuine heart communication with him, then the music becomes less important. Sure, it is great to have the music we like, but as we grow as Christians, we are able to look deeper, and see that blessing God by focusing on him is more important than our personal preferences in music.

Consider the many ways God is worshiped around the world – with huge pipe organs in Europe's great cathedrals, with drums by Africans and Pacific Islanders, with electric guitars in contemporary Western settings, with the chanting of monks and nuns in monasteries, with rams horn trumpets in Israel, with digeridoos by Australian aboriginals, and with tambourines, accordions, flutes, and many other traditional ethnic instruments.

When we can truly worship God no matter what the music is like, we are free to go to any church, in any country, and be happy to celebrate God's goodness without being put off by music that does not connect with us.

In fact, I am convinced that we can only really understand the depth of what worship is when we get past relying on music we like, and freely worship in many different ways, in different cultures, languages, traditions and musical styles. Only then can we begin to distinguish between culture and worship.

Worship must have a container, a way of expressing it, and music and cultural traditions are that container. When we only know one way to worship, we are tempted to think that the container we know is the worship. "If it is not done our way, then it can't be worship." But God is not looking at the container, he is looking at our hearts. We can easily spend so much time making the container pretty that we neglect our hearts.

Jesus said *"First clean the inside of the cup and the plate, that the outside also may be clean."* (Matthew 23:26). We could also say that our worship is like electricity and it needs a wire to travel along. When the wire is connected to a power source, electricity flows. Without the power source, the wire is unable to achieve its purpose of carrying electricity. It is just a wire. Does it matter how beautiful the wire is? No. Its value is measured by how well it carries the power.

When we are not blessed by the music, we have a unique opportunity to worship God free of any emotional attachments to the songs. This kind of worship is sweet to God's ears. Our emotions can easily get entangled with sentimental or nostalgic attachments to songs. We might get warm feelings from the memories prompted by the music, but there are no such temptations when we don't even like the music. We have an opportunity to experience the real meaning of worship, untainted by musical distraction.

When our hearts connect with the ideas being expressed in the songs, we are worshiping in truth. Jesus taught us this kind of worship really blesses God. After all, is that not our desire?

The next time a worship team plays music you don't like, look for meaning in the lyrics and express that to God. Maybe the lyrics offend you, too! Just communicate what is on your heart and God will be blessed. It is him we want to please, right?

Lyrics Are Not Just Words

When we are singing songs, let us consider the lyrics, taking time to ponder what is being communicated. Is it an encouragement to praise, is it an expression of love or commitment, is it remembering the past works of the Lord? When we do this we are able sing with understanding.

When we understand what we are singing and mean the words, then we are going a long way towards being "true" worshipers – the "kind" of worshipers God is looking for. *To mean what we sing, we have to at least understand what we are singing.*

I studied the lyrics in the Psalms to better understand what the writers were communicating. To discern what they were really saying I had to examine each word. It seemed a bit like the time I pulled apart a motorcycle engine for some extensive maintenance, then reassembled it. I understood the motorcycle a lot more after that exercise! When we look at the ideas expressed in the Psalms, we learn Bible-style communication. The Psalms give us a language to express our thoughts and feelings to God in many and varied ways.

Here are a few of the types of communication I saw in the Psalms:

Different ideas to express to God in our praise and worship times – the meaning

Lament – telling God how you feel, a cry from your heart. There are not many contemporary songs that express negative feelings and it is probably not the best idea to get a whole congregation to sing negatively. But it is very helpful and biblical for us to express our frustrations privately to God and receive his comfort.

Exhortation/encouragement – stirring yourself and others to thank or praise. Sometimes we just need a "kick in the pants" to get us into worship, and we see this in the Psalms. A lot of our songs do this, but remember, encouraging people to praise is not praise.

Remembering/thanksgiving – recalling God's past blessings, expressing appreciation. Probably the most important act of God to remember is Jesus' death and resurrection, the greatest demonstration of love the world has seen.

Praise – Saying what God is like. Speaking out the nature and character of God draws our minds to consider his love and holiness. This draws our hearts closer.

Adoration – showing strong affection

Surrender – expressing your allegiance, loyalty and devotion

Awe, wonder – overwhelmed by the aspects of God we cannot comprehend

Love – speaking of God as our deepest desire

When our hearts are filled with love, praise or adoration, we want to express these somehow. The Bible lists a number of different ways to communicate our hearts.

Different ways of expressing our hearts -- the method

Speaking – 1 Chronicles 16:9, Psalm 9:1, 40:5, 105:2

Singing - Exodus 15:1, 2 Samuel 25:50, 1 Chronicles 16:9, Psalm 9:2, 13:6, 27:6, Isaiah 42:10, Jeremiah 20:13, Zechariah 2:10, James 5:13, Hebrews 2:12, 1 Corinthians 14:15, Romans 15:9

Musical instruments – Psalm 150:4, 1 Samuel 18:6, 2 Samuel 6:5, 1 Chronicles 15:16, 16:42, 2 Chronicles 5:13, 7:6, Nehemiah 12:36

Raising hands – Nehemiah 8:6, Psalm 28:2, 63:4, 134:2, 141:2

Kneeling – 2 Chronicles 6:13, Psalm 95:6

Bowing – Genesis 24:26, Exodus 4:31, Matthew 8:2, 9:18, Mark 5:6

Dancing – Exodus 15:20, 2 Samuel 6:14, Psalm 149:3, 150:4, Jeremiah 31:13, Lamentations 5:15

~

THESE BIBLICAL EXPRESSIONS are not confined to one generation or people group, they are universal; we all praise, we all thank. Methods of expressing praise, like singing and music are found in most cultures. But the types of language and styles of music have varied widely around the world and throughout history. The meanings will not change but the methods will.

As each new generation looks to find their sound of worship, one thing will remain the same. God's love and truth will stand the test of time. We need variety in our music, but God's timeless truths of thanks, praise and worship, found in God's Word, will be true everywhere. ***These principles are signposts to guide us along the journey to God's presence.***

So how do we put these principles into action? That's the subject of the final section, "Navigating our Worship." We will investigate some possible ways to follow the signposts. Wise leadership is needed to distinguish biblical principles from cultural norms. Failure has resulted in worship wars and the suppression of indigenous worship sounds (which we examine in a later chapter).

PART III

NAVIGATING OUR WORSHIP

15

WHICH ROUTE TO CHOOSE?

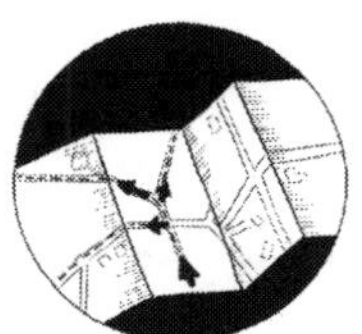

When I use my phone to get street directions, the GPS app will often show different routes to the same destination. Sometimes the shortest is not the best, sometimes the longer route might be quicker. In the end I decide what might work best for me, providing it is legal and I don't go the wrong way down a one-way street.

God has given us principles to follow in worship but there could be a number of routes to travel, whether by traditional liturgies, using contemporary music styles, combinations of both or other ways.

Is it right that new generations sing totally new songs with different styles of music than their parents? Or are they supposed to sing hymns written only in the 18th and 19th centuries? I have often wondered why that older generation who favored these hymns did not sing the songs of the 6th century. I believe each generation needs to write their own songs, but it is also wise to honor the saints of old and to occasionally use songs from the past to keep us connected to the family of God through the ages. We can be inspired by hearing the lyrics of those touched by God over the centuries.

God certainly has bigger "ears" than us. He loves to hear the heart cries of each generation and every people group on the earth. I am convinced he is not as concerned with how it sounds as we are. We would be wise to concentrate on the aspects of worship that God thinks are important; honesty and integrity flowing from pure hearts that express God's truth in God's way.

Although God is not concerned as much about the form of worship, we still have to decide what format and style our worship will follow. Whenever a group of Christians gather to meet with God, a pastor or leadership group decides how they will achieve their aim.

It is certainly not easy to deal with the rapid changes we have seen in the last few decades. The challenges have been met with varying success. Some have overcome through wise leadership, others have lapsed into the worship wars. There is no simple formula to accommodate traditional and contemporary styles.

When a brand new church is planted, the leadership are free to create however they feel God is leading them, usually starting with matching the style to their target group. But well established churches have traditions that can not easily be changed without careful guidance.

God does not need us all to be the same, and a variety of traditions reflect God's nature. He is Three in One and Creator. Unity, diversity and creativity.

But even though our formats may be diverse, unity comes through following biblical principles, foundational understandings that will be true everywhere. The task ahead is to not lose sight of biblical truth in our quest to change or be more "relevant." Is God more impressed with an organ or a guitar? Neither, he is impressed with those who love him and tell the truth about who he is and what he has done.

So, what style is best? That depends on what your purpose is. Evangelistic meetings targeting the unsaved might require a different style than a worship gathering for mature Christians. The best style is the one most appropriate to achieving your main goal.

My journey in the Contemporary Worship Movement has encouraged me to seek biblical basis for the new things we found ourselves doing. Is the music too loud? Is rock music OK? Why don't you sing hymns anymore? As we faced these questions, we found some biblical answers, but radical culture changes produced more challenges. We had to learn by experience.

The next few chapters are a collection of observations and practical experience gained in the context of the CWM. This section is directed more towards worship leaders but remains helpful for all those wanting to experience the presence of God in worship.

May you have the wisdom to sort out not only what applies in your own situation, but also what might be a biblical principle for all time in all situations.

16

FOCUSING ON THE DESTINATION

Awakening worship

Sometimes worship feels a lot like a concert, a team of musicians singing to us while we listen. But the job of a worship leader is not to deliver worship at people, it is to provide an opportunity for the worship of the people to emerge. It is to awaken and encourage their personal expressions of love and adoration. Then it becomes a symphony of praise, an expression from the group. To do this well, we have to be familiar with those we are leading; their level of spiritual maturity; their current experience of difficulties or joy; what might be hindering their freedom. Then we can minister life through songs with identifiable and applicable lyrics.

We shouldn't choose songs just because they might sound good to us. We sing the ones that say what needs to be said at any given time. That, of course, requires we find out what God wants to say, and find lyrics that convey those thoughts. When our worship team is practicing, we should be thinking of how truths are being expressed in the song, not just whether we are playing the right chords and rhythms. It is far too easy to spend most of our time on the music and forget the importance of the words. I often encourage worship leaders to ***"lead with the truth, not the music!"***

Leading with the truth means that we focus on how the scripture-based lyrics draw us to God rather than aiming primarily for an emotional response using pleasing melodies and rhythms. Good worship songs have a powerful message that is readily understood and accepted, even by people who don't like the music we play. We can bring unity by expressing the timeless truths from God's Word. Truth plus music is a powerful combination, we need both for our songs to work.

It is Not Your Gig

A friend of mine once said: "Worship is too important a ministry to be left to musicians." At first I thought, "How rude!" I then began to understand the truth hidden behind this paradox. Worship music needs to be music that best fits the people we are leading. It is music "of the people," not music for the musicians. Worship times are not the platform for us musicians to demonstrate our instrumental ability. The music we play is not composed primarily to satisfy our creative juices; it is for the purpose of helping the people express their hearts to God. Worship music must be within the abilities of the people to follow and sing. Our musical talents are usually further ahead than the rest of the people, that's why we are in the team! But this role also means that we might not get all the musical enjoyment that we desire. We are not to judge the music by concert standards, but by its ability to capture people's imaginations, drawing out heartfelt praise and worship.

So, in a sense, it is likely we may have to "dial down" our musical aspirations and abilities to match those of the average person in the congregation. This may be hard to accept, and it appears to be contrary to all we have heard about "musical excellence." But we must realize that *excellence is about doing the best job at fulfilling the intended purpose.* Excellent worship music helps the people express themselves. Sometimes a simple song does that best. Don't begin by measuring a worship song by its musical qualities, firstly evaluate its ability to draw people to worship.

God wants us to try our best with music, but music is not worship. We need to be trained in the specific skills needed in worship leading, not just in music. Excellence in worship has a different set of criteria to excellence in music.

In 1 Chronicles 15:22 we see Chenaniah as the leader of the musicians because he was skilled. The Hebrew word for skill used here does not just mean technical skill in music. It also has the sense of wisdom and understanding, knowing what is going on and knowing the right thing to do. Skill in worship is understanding what is happening and knowing what to do and when to do it. God will definitely use our musical skill. I have always encouraged worship leaders to practice all they can, not because they need to sound professional, but to be able to concentrate less on how well they're playing and more on what God is saying and how he is leading.

The more songs we know, both as an individual and as a team, the more we are able to use songs not on our set list. In other words, *the more we are prepared, the more we can be spontaneous!* God wants to teach us another kind of skill– how to gather a group in raising genuine praise and worship to God. As we recognize the difference between musical and worship skills, we guard ourselves against letting music become our main concern during our worship. If music becomes the main thing, we lose sight of where we are going and what God wants to achieve.

Music... the Master?

In his early recording days, contemporary worship pioneer David Garratt was encouraged by his piano player to develop his group's music beyond their simple three-chord, four-line choruses. This offer from a skillful, but non-believing musician, appealed to David and the team. They were not trained musicians or singers themselves, so they welcomed his expert help. But later on, in a subtle way, David felt they were replacing their mandate with a challenge to create music that would impress people rather than draw them to Jesus. During that time, the band noticed a few disturbing trends . . .

• The harmonies the piano player taught were complicated and people could not follow or learn the songs easily.

• The songs he wrote, while musically interesting, were too complex. The team felt they had lost their simplicity.

• They had given the final decision making to a man who did not share their vision.

• It did not seem God was blessing these efforts.

• Thankfully, the recording sank without a trace.

David felt the music had become the master and not the servant. Their experience is a warning for all of us who minister in worship leading. The music, and the musician, should never become the master. When our trust is in a man or woman, rather than God, we forfeit our dependence on him.

In our worship practices we often spend way more time practicing the music than seeking God's plan. If the worship leader just tells the band what they're to do, they are not involved in the process of hearing God about the direction of the meeting. They are then tempted to become more focused on the music than on God's direction. Music can easily become the whole object of our efforts.

So we need to understand where we are going and how to get there. Understanding the role of music will help keep us focused on the journey of worship into the presence of God. There is one skill that becomes very important in this process – being led by the Holy Spirit, hearing God's voice in leading us. We explore what this might mean in the next chapter.

17

THE HOLY SPIRIT GUIDES US

One of the most important lessons I have learned about leading worship is to be led by the Holy Spirit. Most of us would agree with this, but what does it mean? It is helpful to see what the Bible says about the role of the Holy Spirit.

Just before Jesus went up to heaven, he reassured his disciples that they wouldn't be left alone. He promised that another "friend" would come to be with them. They had been with Jesus for three years, hearing him preach, seeing healings and other miracles. What an amazing time that must have been! But they did not fully understand what Jesus prophesied. Even after he rose from the dead, they still had no idea what Pentecost might bring.

Jesus promised the Holy Spirit would come soon after he left. The Holy Spirit was to be their companion, just as Jesus had been, as friend, counselor, teacher and encourager. At Pentecost the power of God fell on those gathered; suddenly timidity and fear seemed a thing of the past. Peter preached in power. He and other apostles healed the sick, spoke in tongues and prophesied. Jesus had passed on his work to people just like us! The promise was not just to the disciples alive then, it was for all who followed.

When Jesus was on earth, he talked with the disciples face to face, but we don't have Jesus with us here, speaking to us like that. Those gathered in the Upper Room at Pentecost had a dramatic introduction to the new way God was going to speak and lead them. The Holy Spirit led the apostles in the Book of Acts. We can also be led this way, by listening to the Spirit's promptings. Every Christian has to learn how to hear and communicate to God. We don't usually learn this in public school. Sometimes we are not even taught it in church! It is just like talking to a friend, but then again, it is also different, because Jesus is not here physically like our earthly friends.

Hearing God's voice is foundational in developing a friendship with God. So often we talk to God but don't learn to listen. A relationship is two-way. We know that having a friend means we talk to them, and hear from them. How does someone become our best friend? It is usually because they've confided in us. If we are not hearing from God, is it really a relationship? It may be just an admiration from afar. The Bible is full of stories of men and women who heard from God. Jesus said "My sheep hear my voice." If we are one of his sheep, then we can expect to hear his voice. Growing in a relationship with God not only means talking to him, it involves hearing from him.

We apply the same listening ear to what God might be saying in our preparation and leading worship. We must make time to settle our busy minds and listen for his direction.

One typical approach to leading worship would be to get some helpful input from our pastor or leader about the theme for the meeting. Then we begin to search our list of songs for those we think might be appropriate. All this is helpful, but is it enough? Without a word from God, we are left with our own understanding. Proverbs 3:4-5 says:

> *"Trust in the Lord with all your heart, and do not lean on your own understanding. In all your ways acknowledge him, and he will make straight your paths."*

I compiled a large song database on my laptop and it was a very useful tool, but now we have specially designed worship software along with the ability to search YouTube and Google. But I still pray and ask God to guide me, even as I use these tools. I consider the lyrics while listening and wait for a sense that the Holy Spirit is highlighting a particular song.

When we believe we have heard from God, or felt his leading, then it is up to us to obey. We can never be totally sure it is God until we step out in faith and believe him for the results. God blesses faith, and faith requires that we hear from him.

As I was leading a worship song in a YWAM meeting in Auckland, New Zealand, I felt the prompting of God to keep playing the chord sequence of the chorus. Usually we go through our set list with intros and finishes all arranged. When we hear God ask us to deviate from the plan, it is a test of faith. I kept the chord sequence going and began to sing out spontaneously my own melody. There was an immediate response as I felt a groundswell of participation. It was as though the whole room came together in united praise, even though there was no set melody or lyrics. I was tempted to stop when it died down a little, but I felt God was saying to keep the chord sequence going. The volume rose and fell a number of times, but an amazing sense of God's presence remained. It went on like this for 45 minutes. How could one chord sequence last for so long? Didn't we all get bored? No.

When God's presence comes like that, we feel a touch of heaven on earth! When we learn to hear his voice or sense his leading, then obey in faith, we can truly say that the Holy Spirit is leading our worship.

The danger of doing our own thing

If we are not being led by the Holy Spirit, we open ourselves to the temptation to please people or to rely on our own limited perspective. We can easily slip into pride, especially if we are talented and people love what we do. Failure to seek God's leading is a recipe for defeat as the children of Israel discovered, with drastic consequences. Like the Pharisees that Jesus rebuked, we may look and sound good on the outside, but if we are not communicating with God, hearing his voice, we begin to lose relationship. We become religious!

We do what we think is best. We find ourselves saying: "I know what to do, I'm experienced!" We end up leading "default" worship, the kind we lead when there is no creativity springing from God's word to us. It becomes a chore. Sometimes I have found myself saying "I *have* to lead worship tonight." One time, as I said this, I felt the Lord correct me. I had been treating worship leading as an obligation and not as a privilege. A new phrase came to me: "I *get* to lead worship tonight!" What a difference that simple statement made!

After serving God in missions for a number of years, at one time I realized I lacked enthusiasm as I prepared for another School of Worship. I sat in my office and cried out to God. I began hearing a song being played in the next office. The words began to speak to me. The song repeated the words "light the fire again." That was exactly what my heart craved, more fire, more passion! As I identified with those lyrics I felt a wave of God's Spirit stirring passion again, I began breathing deeply. It was like I was breathing in God's breath, his life, and I felt like he was filling me again. Later during that school we saw a remarkable move of God as he touched most of the staff and students in powerful ways. Without re-firing we grow cold. At that time I needed some new fire.

Hearing from God, waiting for his creativity to spring up within us, keeps us enthusiastic as the "springs of life" well up from deep in our hearts. Jesus promised that rivers of living water would spring up from within us as the Holy Spirit worked.

> *"Whoever believes in me, as the Scripture has said, Out of his heart will flow rivers of living water.'" Now this he said about the Spirit, whom those who believed in him were to receive" – John 7:38-39*

> *My son, be attentive to my words; incline your ear to my sayings.*
> *Let them not escape from your sight; keep them within your heart.*
> *For they are* ***life*** *to those who find them, and healing to all their flesh.*
> *Keep your heart with all vigilance, for from it flow the* ***springs of life****. – Proverbs 4:20-23*

A heart connected to God, hearing from him and experiencing his love daily, is the spring that keeps us fresh. So how does the Holy Spirit guide us when we are leading worship?

18

HOW TO FOLLOW THE LEADING?

Here are a few thoughts about one of the most important aspects of worship leading. We need to keep listening to the prompting of God's Spirit . . .

1. When We Prepare . . .

Ask God to lead you to a theme. A song may come to mind, or a verse of scripture. Remember, it is about expressing the truth, not about enjoying the music!

When we seek God for direction, we are able to lead with a confidence that only the "word of the Lord" can bring. It is not what I want, but what God wants.

It is better if you can listen to God in a team. If we can seek God as a group, we gain a sense of safety and blessing flowing from the unity among the members. We are more confident in what God has said, and the team is enabled to focus more on God's word rather than on the music only.

Because we often have our own opinions about the worship time, it is a good idea to admit this before God in prayer by confessing our need to hear his heart and not just our own thoughts. Then we trust God to lead and guide us.

2. When We Are Leading . . .

Not Rushing on

I have found it helpful to avoid jumping quickly from song to song. There are times when it is helpful to wait, maybe playing quietly in the background as we ponder the truth of the song or to say a quick, silent prayer, asking God if he has any leading that might be different from our set plan. I was leading a few songs after teaching in a YWAM school in Australia, when I felt that I should not launch into another song but play quietly and trust God to work in the students' lives. I obeyed that prompting but my faith was challenged because I could not see much happening. I continued only because I sensed it was what God wanted. As we waited in the quiet suddenly one of the students began sobbing, then another, and soon the staff began ministering God's comfort and healing to many in the class. Afterwards the leader of the school encouraged me by saying the staff had been praying for a breakthrough in emotional healing amongst the students. Times like this have taught me that although we have a responsibility to listen and step out in faith, it is the work of the Holy Spirit that touches lives. If we follow his leading, he does marvelous things.

Sensing something

One morning as I began a class at our training center in Makapala, Hawaii, I had the students express in prayer their desire to know God in a deeper way. I played some recorded worship songs over their sound system as they prayed. I soon began to sense the presence of God in the room, a feeling of peace and of anticipation that God was about to begin answering their prayers. God promises us that if we seek him, we will find him.

I played song after song from my laptop and for the next eighty minutes we witnessed the wonder of God's working amongst a group of students hungry for God's presence. Some bowed low or kneeled, some began dancing with joy, some prayed blessing on others, some received God's touch with tears of joy and others began praying for nations while placing their hands on the world map. Later as I viewed photographs taken by one of the students, I was amazed how they captured the intensity of the responses to the moving of God's Spirit.

A word or phrase pops into our mind

Sometimes a phrase may come to mind which we may sense is the voice of God. Experience, like trial and error, is one way we learn to distinguish this voice from our own desires. If we think it is God, obey that voice and see what happens. I have tried this may times and found I became more confident in deciding whether the voice in my mind was God or just me.

I once was struggling with leading a worship song, it just was not working. I heard a voice say: "stop the song and pray." It is a little unusual to do that but I was thinking it might be God's voice. I stopped the song and announced: "Hey everyone, I don't think this is working!" I thought I had blown it! You don't usually say things like that when leading worship. But it sure grabbed their attention. So we all prayed and the atmosphere changed. People who had seemed aloof or bored before now became engaged. Stopping the song was a little awkward, but it showed me the importance of obeying that still small voice.

Trust God or die!

There are times when we, for one reason or another, are unable to prepare for every occurrence in a worship time. We might have no time to practice, a musician suddenly is unable to come, or the electricity fails. Once I had to lead a large group in an auditorium that did not open until a few minutes before our start time. We had to run in, set up the sound equipment and launch into our songs with very little time to do a sound check. God blessed us in worship despite the difficult circumstances. It is times like these when we can not control everything that we are forced to trust that God will work for good, no matter what the situation.

It may even be to our advantage to voluntarily put ourselves in the position of having to trust God like Jonathan and his armor bearer did.

> *"Jonathan said to the young man who carried his armor, 'Come, let us go over to the garrison of these uncircumcised. It may be that the Lord will work for us, for nothing can hinder the Lord from saving by many or by few.'" – 1 Samuel 14:6*

I once found myself designated as the main worship leader for a YWAM Discipleship Training School. As I had done this before, I knew how challenging it was to be the only musician on our staff, to plan a 30-minute worship time each week day for three months. I felt a little discouraged at the prospect of doing this again. I prayed for a solution and sensed I had an answer.

I asked the others on staff if we could change the worship

schedule to just two mornings a week but to allow 90 minutes. This left us time to allow the Holy Spirit to begin to go deeper into our lives. I had to trust God to break into our worship, because I certainly could not keep enthusiasm going for that long with a few songs. It was a situation of "trust God or die!"

As I look back on that school, I remember how God ministered to students and staff alike in ways that I had not seen in our 30-minute sessions. I can recall students being set free from bondages, others sensing God's presence like never before. One in particular who wept as God touched him, left a small puddle of tears on the linoleum floor. I can only imagine how much God was moved by that little pool which demonstrated such softness towards him!

3. Afterwards – Evaluating

Do you have the courage to ask God what he thought of what you did? Or do you as a worship leader hang on every compliment given by people?

Our School of Worship in Kona, Hawaii, began questioning whether evaluation is a biblical principle. In Genesis we read how God observed his creation, and he saw that it was good! So we went ahead and looked for ways to evaluate our progress in discipling worship leaders.

We assigned our students the task of leading the class in worship and then took time to evaluate the team. We did not realize what a risky business this was! We offended some in the process, but our mistakes taught us about what criteria to use to evaluate in a constructive way.

After one student-led worship time, we began a class discussion, inviting the students' evaluation of their worship time.

One after another the students revealed their thoughts. Unfortunately, there were too many mistakes pointed out. They were not happy with all the negativity and as the one responsible for the class, I was not either. It led me to ask God what we were doing wrong. As I sought the Lord I felt him say we were all evaluating on the basis of our own opinions, and nobody had asked God what he thought! We concentrated mostly on musical evaluation and not on whether we had met with God or sensed his presence.

As I pondered this, I realized how easy it is to be concerned with what people think. Many times when I led worship I would have one or two come to me and say how much they enjoyed the time. Of course that made me feel good, but I began to wonder whether this was as significant as I had thought. Who was I trying to please anyway? So I began to ask God his opinion after leading worship. The first time I did this, as I asked God, I felt his whisper: "Did you do everything I asked you to do? Did you listen to me and obey?" It seemed so simple. God was not asking me to please people or make them feel happy, he was simply asking me to listen and obey. If I did that then I was successful and God was pleased with me. It felt so freeing.

From then on, we were more careful in how we evaluated our worship teams. We would pause and ask God what he thought. We would still look at some practical aspects of leading worship such as song selection, musicianship, etc., but we would concentrate on the most important issues. Did God speak? Did we sense the presence of the Holy Spirit? Did the team hear and obey God's leading?

From then on, I would ask God what he thought of any worship time I led. Whether people told me they enjoyed the time or not, I would get by myself, and ponder whether the things I did were what God had led me to do. Did I do anything that was not out of love and obedience to him? Was there any part of me that was trying to impress people?

This helped war against one of the biggest enemies worship leaders face, the spirit of the Pharisees, impressing people by putting on a show. Worship involves humbling ourselves, which is why pride is perhaps the biggest enemy of true worship, especially if it is found in the worship team members.

19

DEVELOPING SENSITIVITY TO THE HOLY SPIRIT

Not everyone senses God's leading in the same way; we must train our own ears to hear and our own eyes to see what God may be saying or doing. Here are a few possibilities that might help.

Reading God's Word

Ask God what he is saying to you, don't just read or analyze the words. As we soak ourselves with the truth of who God is and what he does, we develop a biblical language of praise and worship. The Psalms are so important in helping us gain a language of worship.

After a while I had learned by heart a number of biblical phrases of worship and praise that I could spontaneously speak out in appropriate times. They did not have to be long passages. There is power in speaking God's Word aloud and it certainly keeps us close to the truth in worship.

Listening to praise and worship music

As I listen to recorded songs, I usually ask myself whether the songs are touching only my emotions, or is there something deeper. I relax and enjoy the songs, learning to sense how the song ministers to me and how it might work in leading others. These times are not only precious times with God, but also helpful training in the skill of choosing songs. As I connect with the heart of the song privately, it becomes easier to be genuine when I lead the song publicly. When my heart is in the song, people recognize it. Our connection to the song's message is a key to the presence of the Holy Spirit.

Worshiping by Ourselves

We can worship on our own by listening to recorded music or by playing our own instrument and/or singing our own songs to the Lord. It is important to develop a habit of worshiping God by ourselves, away from the responsibility of serving on a worship team. When no one else is around we can be free to be totally concentrated on God, free from the responsibility of leading others, and as a bonus, we are free from worrying about what people think! These times form a solid foundation of authenticity in our public ministry, guarding us against worship becoming just a job.

Praying in the Spirit

In 1 Corinthians 14, Paul encourages us to pray with our understanding and also to pray in the Spirit. This implies that praying in the Spirit is in a different realm than that of the mind. It is in the spirit realm, and Paul is referring to praying in a God-given language not understood by the speaker, commonly called "praying in tongues."

This gift has been maligned over the centuries, probably because the enthusiasm expressed by a few zealous ones can easily overwhelm those who are more reserved. It is also somewhat of an offense to those dominated only by reason and intellectual argument. This is unfortunate, because this gift is so powerful. Paul said he wished that all would speak in tongues.

Some have said they don't feel the need for this gift. But Paul clearly commands us in 1 Corinthians 14:1 to "earnestly desire spiritual gifts." We might not all receive the same way, but perhaps it might be wise to listen to Paul and at least desire the gift!

To those who speak in tongues; God does not take gifts back, nor does he give gifts to put on the shelf and say, "yeah, I did that once!" Keep speaking. Tongues build us up and we certainly need that. It works! I find it helps me get more spiritually aware, especially when I am walking by myself. I love to use the time to communicate in the spirit realm with my Savior.

I think the process of receiving the gift of tongues by faith is helpful in increasing our faith for other supernatural working of the Holy Spirit, like healing and miracles. The requirement is stepping out in faith and obedience, believing we have what we are asking. Trusting in God's Word is the key. We have our part, opening our mouths and believing that we will receive what God has promised, while God does his part, filling us with a new language in the Spirit. We can't reason our way to these gifts!

To receive the gift of tongues, we have to overcome two lingering doubts, both of which hinder our ability to receive. We might tell ourselves "it is just me!" or "it sounds weird!" We can easily discourage ourselves with these thoughts. Our minds are often offended, but when we sense the surge of the Spirit of God, we realize there is something deeper going on!

Hindrances to Being Led by the Holy Spirit

Trying to Please People

A desire to impress our audience is one of the biggest traps for those ministering in worship. We have to settle the question in our hearts, "Am I trying to please God or people?" When pleasing God is our aim, it won't matter if he asks us to do something unusual. Once I felt God say to me that I should encourage the congregation to give a loud victory shout. I was not sure why God would ask me to do that, and I worried, "What will they think of me?" As I kept singing, the thought wouldn't go away, so I got up the courage to step out in faith and give the opportunity to shout! Would it be just a loud noise or would there be a release of freedom in the spirit? I did not know the answer to that question. That's what faith is all about.

We hear a leading from God and without knowing how it will turn out, we obey God and step out in faith. As the people shouted, a wave of freedom and victory filled the room. I could not tell what it meant for each individual, but I knew something was happening as we lifted up our voices. I might have offended someone's idea of reverence for God, I don't know. But fearing what people think is a sure way to become ineffective in worship. Let's please God by obeying him, no matter what our fears try to tell us.

Confidence in our own Talents

"We sound good tonight!" I have thought that at times, but I have learned not to trust in that approach. God has surprised me many times when we have practiced well and put too much confidence in what we have got to offer. Sometimes our worship has fallen flat, and the Lord has reminded me I had trusted too much in our team's talents. Other times he has blessed a worship time when we have had little time to practice. I am not saying we should neglect practice, but through these experiences, God has shown me that success in worship is his domain. We have to listen and obey, then the results are up to him. We do the possible, and God does the impossible, the things that only he can do.

Confidence in our own Experience

The longer we lead, the more experienced we become, and therefore we are tempted in our pride to say, "I know what to do!" The more success we have, the greater the danger to rely on our own skills. Experience should lead us to be even more focused on what God is saying, not on what we think would work. It is too easy to let our experience guide us. God blesses faith, and faith comes by hearing from him, so listening and obeying should be the hallmark of a skillful worship leader.

Planning that Does Not Allow for Flexibility

If every minute of our time allowed is scheduled, there is a great temptation to believe that we have it all together. It is necessary to plan, but keep listening to God. He may have given us the plan, but it never hurts to keep listening to the promptings of the Holy Spirit, our hearing from God in our planning is rarely 100% accurate.

Being Pushed for Time

Sometimes we might be tempted to rush through a song set, because we have practiced songs and we really want to sing them. If you have been given a shorter timeframe, don't try to pack in too many songs. Always leave time for the Holy Spirit to extend whatever direction in worship you had planned. It is also important to respect the time frame allowed. It is very easy for worship leaders to go over time when things are going well. I tell our students that they must look to the meeting leader for permission to go further. Often a leader has signaled to me to carry on. Then it is OK. I would half-jokingly advise that God's blessing stops as soon as we disregard the leader's instructions. It might actually be true!

Swinging Between Spontaneity and Planning

Sometimes we swing between two extremes. One group might say, "We just let the Holy Spirit lead us." That sounds spiritual, but it generally leads to sameness, and a lack of creativity. It is sometimes an excuse for laziness. There is also a lot of pressure to come up with something when the mind goes blank. This leads to what might be called "production anxiety." We have to come up with something on the spot because there has been no planning. This type of approach usually is a knee-jerk reaction to those who plan every small detail in worship. They can feel restricted and inflexible, and in response, they reject all planning.

Those who have been in unplanned services have sensed the insecurity of not knowing what is happening or where the meeting is going. They might then respond by planning and organizing, bringing a sense of security and relaxation, not having to think all the time, "What do I do now?"

Wisdom is a balance between these two extremes. Life flows from the tension between spontaneity and planning. Extreme planning will kill life, but so does total spontaneity.

If we have planned every detail, then there is a huge temptation to relax and not listen to God's voice at all, or even be open to a new idea of our own, or to make any mid-course corrections. If we are totally spontaneous, we are making the assumption that God cannot speak or lead us until the meeting starts. God is able to lead us before and during a meeting! This is the basis for allowing both planning and spontaneity – God's ability to speak any time we are willing to listen to his guidance.

Once again, Spirit-led worship boils down to hearing God, which in turn relies on daily relationship with him. Anyone can learn principles and rules of worship leading. But life does not flow from obeying the rules, it flows from relationship with God.

20

LET MY PEOPLE GO!

David and Dale Garratt have been pioneers in the Contemporary Worship Movement. Their Scripture in Song ministry produced albums and songbooks that captured the sounds of a new generation. Through their music, many young people encountered God powerfully and learned to worship him with musical styles different from their parents' generation.

My own worship leading has benefited from their ministry example. They followed God's direction to "lead the people to me" rather than just singing *about* him. And a generation followed.

After David and Dale had traveled the world teaching and leading worship, God led them back to their native New Zealand. They were challenged to learn how they could help enable indigenous peoples worship God with a freedom suppressed since colonial days. David's insights provide valuable principles for those involved with cross-cultural worship.

In an interview with David, he recounted how God led him

to embrace cultural expressions of worship often considered unacceptable in the church.

"When we began Scripture in Song, the idea of cultural differences never occurred to us at all. We were influenced by two things, the music we heard on the radio at that time, and the music played in churches. But the organ music in churches was not touching the younger generation.

"In 1968 we decided to produce recordings using a rhythm section, and from there it escalated. Our ministry grew as we produced albums and song books which sold widely around the English speaking world.

"Then, in 1986, God gave me a revelation. We Westerners need revelation to get us thinking and acting outside our culture; it doesn't happen naturally. It happened this time while I was away at a retreat for songwriters, and it is still such a vivid memory for me. We were walking along a beach, and out of the blue the word "culture" came straight into my mind. Then, following that, I heard "if you are going to be fully effective in this nation, you will have to understand the culture of the indigenous Maori people."

"So I visited a number of Maori marae (meeting places) and listened to the elders. I found that whenever an issue or problem came up, I would want to give an answer I thought they needed to hear. I was beginning to recognize the dominance of my own culture, and I realized I had to stop this tendency to have all the answers. I knew I had to begin listening. I was from a dominant culture and I had to heed the wisdom of these people and learn from them.

"I began listening and wondered how our nation's history might have been different if the English missionaries had recognized that not everything about Maori culture was evil. If only they had learned the wonderful qualities the Maori culture possessed, and learned from them. I saw in them the value of extended family, of honoring elders, caring for children that are not their own and the unifying value of doing things together. I understood that we Westerners are culturally so independent. If only the first white Christians had seen some of the good along with the obvious idolatry and paganism.

"I have since had a number of experiences in other places, confirming what I had learned. Each of these examples had a significant influence on me, showing me the huge misunderstandings and tensions there are between different cultural groups. I also saw how difficult it is for believers of different cultural backgrounds to trust each other enough to work together in a leadership context. Inevitably it seems the dominant culture takes over. However, even though it is extremely difficult, I still believe a genuine unity in diversity between God's people is on his heart.

Aboriginals in Australia - once forgotten sounds given back to God

"I once attended a conference in Alice Springs, in the center of Australia at the invitation of Christian Aboriginals. I went with a small group of musicians and was asked to speak in the morning sessions.

"The way they conducted their meetings closely followed a Western model. They played guitars, spoke only in English, and did not bring any of their traditional instruments. When they preached, they sounded like old-time Pentecostals. The Aboriginals are a gentle people, so this fiery preaching appeared uncharacteristic. It seemed this is how they assumed Christians were to behave. It made me wonder how much of their culture remained hidden.

"So, in the morning session, I encouraged them to bring their precious cultural uniqueness, and offer it to their Creator in worship. As I spoke and sang our songs, I felt little connection with them. Then, on the final morning, two of the Aboriginal men came in with pieces of plastic piping. They stood at the back of the room, playing the piping, imitating their own instrument, the didgeridoo.

"We invited them to come to the front and keep playing. I soon noticed two things.

"Firstly, the sounds did not blend well with our music. Secondly, the Aboriginal people came alive as they heard those sounds. When I saw this, I realized this journey was more than including a few cultural items in our worship. It went much deeper, right to the core of who these people are. A sound that was life to them. I wondered whether hearing that sound in a Christian context had ever been considered. Because they had only seen Christianity within the framework of Western culture, they had put aside their own celebrations as not being Christian. But the sound of the didgeridoo was deeply ingrained in their souls. These sounds were waiting to be released and given as wholehearted expressions to God.

"I longed to see these cultural songs and dances in the church, so my initial reaction was to encourage them to use their instruments in worship to God. I then realized I had to step back a little. If I pushed too much, I could be doing the reverse of what my forefathers had done by forbidding these sounds. If I gave advice, which they might follow, then I would be placing them in another box, forcing an expression on them, rather than letting it come from within."

Tonga - freedom to worship beyond church traditions

"I was speaking in a YWAM school in Tonga. Gathered in the tent were people from different regions of the world; South Americans, Africans, Polynesians. Some say music is a universal language, but Westerners can take this to mean that everyone should like the same music. I have found that Africans, South Americans and Polynesians each respond to different rhythms and music.

"God showed me the importance of learning to accommodate different groups so they can wholeheartedly express their worship, especially in a multi-cultural environment. A Samoan musician in the school expressed to me his desire to praise God in new ways. He did not want to be expected to perform a typically Samoan song or dance. He wanted to be free to express it in his own way, which may or may not sound Samoan. The same Holy Spirit in us all, can draw out varied expressions which demonstrate the different facets of God's character.

"In that class was a young woman from the Philippines who began to dance beautifully during the free worship time. During the lunch break I asked her where she had learned the dance. She told me that she had never learned it. She went on to explain that it was a part of who she was, it was something coming from deep within, not carefully rehearsed movements.

"Another time I spoke with a Tongan woman who explained that her people can dance till they reach the door of the church, but they stop dancing as they enter, because this is not accepted in the church. It reinforced in me a recognition that indigenous peoples have had to deny part of their God-given identity when forced to become like Western Christians."

Native Americans in Oregon, USA - one indigenous group inspires another to freedom

"Another time, I was asked to visit a Native American reservation in Oregon. I was accompanied by three Maori from New Zealand. The Native Americans were just beginning to explore the idea that their native sounds and instruments could be used for worship of the one true God. When our men from New Zealand performed a haka (Maori war dance), the freedom with which they expressed their Maori sounds inspired the locals. It connected deep within their spirit. They had been discouraged from using their traditional sounds in the Christian church, but here they saw another group of indigenous people pouring out their hearts with a freedom rarely, if ever, seen in their experience of church. Even though they were from a different culture, they recognized what was happening. The Maori, who were tribal people much like themselves, were using their own sounds to worship God!

South Korea - indigenous and Western sounds together!

"On another occasion, I was asked by some Korean Christians to teach them how to use their traditional instruments in worship. My initial impression of Koreans was that they were formal, polite and definitely not extravagant in their behavior. I began to encourage them to offer to God, in worship, the sounds that he had given them in their culture. They began to dance and sing with great enthusiasm as I just sat back and watched.

"They had been told that using their own instruments was wrong because they had been used in ancestor worship. Now I was encouraging them to offer those instruments in worship to

God. I realized I could be communicating that Western instruments were wrong for them. So I reminded them it was not a matter of using this or that instrument, it was about freedom. What mattered to God was that they would express their hearts to him freely with whatever they had. Instruments were not the issue, and if they could play a traditional instrument in faith then they should do so.

"In this particular room, they had on the stage a bass player, a drummer, a keyboard player and a guitarist along with traditional Korean drums. I noticed that those with indigenous instruments set the tone and rhythm, which was then picked up by the modern instruments. There seemed to be no conflict between the two groups. This confirmed to me that Koreans did not necessarily have to go back to their old music, but still there were distinct sounds that could unlock their hearts and bring an even greater freedom than if they stayed with modern music only."

DAVID GARRATT BELIEVES the Father is searching to reveal a new church model, one not based on known Western ways, but more of a global expression of his body. He sees God wanting many different people groups shining his love as he receives unique celebrations of praise and worship from within those cultures.

There is considerable pressure against this. It is a spiritual conflict where misunderstanding and fear in the church shade us from the light of God's purposes.

"Association with anything indigenous or tribal has always been questioned by the church at large. Unfortunately, our eyes have been blinded to the value God has placed in the people groups of the earth. We have failed to recognize God's spiritual gifts resident in these cultures so we have missed the blessing of new aspects of God's character revealed in their expressions of worship," he says.

David adds: "In the church we haven't really understood that the Creator has gifted the cultures of the world with unique expressions of their own. God never intended everyone to worship in the same way with the same methods and songs. The riches he has placed in every people group make up a glorious symphony echoing heaven as recorded in John's vision. In the book of Revelation, we see the amazing picture of every nation, tribe and tongue worshiping before the throne of God. I am convinced they won't all look or sound the same. One day we'll see it for ourselves, but for now, we have an opportunity to experience a small taste of heaven, as we allow different sounds and rhythms from the nations freely lifting up the name of Jesus."

The lessons David has learned are important for all who desire to see the nations of the earth freed to wholeheartedly worship God in all their cultural uniqueness. The same principles apply when new generations within the same country develop fresh ways of expressing their worship. My journey was not one of ethnic culture, but of generational differences. When a new generation of Christians began to use their new musical sounds in the church, the guardians of the status quo became nervous and resisted them. My story was typical of that season.

With these lessons learned, a new season of free expression of worship is sure to emerge.

21

WHERE TO FROM HERE?

Now that the Contemporary Worship Movement (CWM) has been widely established and accepted throughout the world, we are poised for a fresh move of God's Spirit – a move that will take us further and deeper in our experience of corporate worship. Considering how far we have come in the last few years, I can only imagine the growth of the next 10 to 20 years! God has been pouring out his Spirit on generation after generation and he is not about to stop now. There will be more, probably beyond our expectations. This is what God is like. This is what he has been doing for centuries.

The CWM succeeded in breaking through the stained-glass barrier of church musical tradition to connect with new generations of young people. If we carefully follow the principles of God's Word and live in the freedom of the Spirit, we can expect to embrace new levels of worship. It will arise from committed disciples of Christ whose expressions will genuinely mirror their everyday devotion. They will discover a day-by-day relationship with Jesus far more fulfilling than relying on the occasional emotional highs of big worship gatherings.

We will begin to see radical lovers of Jesus whose lives will not conform to the drifting morality of the surrounding culture.

We will see worshipers able to pour out their struggles honestly. They won't need will-power to coldly "choose" to worship because they will naturally turn to God no matter what the circumstances, no matter how they feel. They will delight to express either joy or sadness knowing they will receive comfort, hope and encouragement in God's presence.

They will be able to worship whether or not they like the music, because they know where the real enjoyment lies, in connecting with God. While encountering unfamiliar worship music, they won't be distracted because they detect a genuine love of God.

They will become tired of religious cliches in their songs, phrases that are well past their use-by date. They will use biblically inspired lyrics to connect truth with their real life experience.

Their thanksgiving will move past just "being thankful" to conscious remembering and declaring what God has been doing in their lives and in the world. Their thanks will build hope for the future because they know that God will keep doing what he has done in the past.

Their praise will reflect a deep knowledge of God's character. They will have more meaningful things to say than the usual "Hallelujah" and "praise the Lord." Songs will begin to speak more directly of what he is like: loving, tender, compassionate, merciful, victorious, powerful and so much more.

Their worship will combine heart-felt adoration along with a genuine submission to his lordship, because Jesus will be Lord all week, not just in worship meetings.

It will become more obvious when worship leaders are

humble servants who understand their worship calling rather than being motivated by popularity or performance. These leaders will draw us into God's presence because they know it themselves. They won't push us towards merely outward expressions by continually urging us to "lift it up," or "sing it out." Their personal engaging with the truth in the songs will draw others into the message. Our response will then flow naturally rather than a forced, polite obedience to the leader's urging.

This kind of worship will achieve more than entertaining an audience, it will take us into a place of rest and refreshing that satisfies our souls and pleases the heart of God.

God has so much more for us. I can hardly wait to see what's next!

ABOUT THE AUTHOR

Kevin Norris has been a teacher and discipler in the area of contemporary worship for over three decades. Originally from New Zealand, he has been a worship leader in the context of the international missions movement, Youth With A Mission (YWAM). He was the director of YWAM's School of Worship in Kona, Hawaii and has developed its global curriculum. He teaches on many YWAM schools across the world and lives in Kona with his wife, Liz, while their three sons, David, Daniel and Jordan and daughter, Kayla, have all been trained and served with YWAM in multiple countries.